D0897912

Fantasy Literature for Children and Young Adults

Pamela S. Gates
Susan B. Steffel
Francis J. Molson

THE SCARECROW PRESS, INC.
Lanham, Maryland, and Oxford
2003

SCARECROW PRESS, INC.

Published in the United States of America
by Scarecrow Press, Inc.
A Member of the Rowman & Littlefield Publishing Group
4501 Forbes Blvd., Suite 200
Lanham, Maryland 20706
www.scarecrowpress.com

PO Box 317
Oxford
OX2 9RU, UK

British Library Cataloguing in Publication Information Available

Library of Congress Cataloging-in-Publication Data

Gates, Pamela S.
   Fantasy literature for children and young adults / Pamela Gates, Susan B. Steffel, Francis J. Molson.
     p. cm.
   Includes bibliographical references and index.
   ISBN 0-8108-4637-3 (alk. paper)
   1. Children's literature—History and criticism. 2. Young adult literature—History and criticism. 3. Fantasy literature—History and criticism. I. Steffel, Susan B. II. Molson, Francis J., 1932– III. Title.
PN1009.A1 G36 2003
809'.89282—dc21   2002151458

♾™ The paper used in this publication meets the minimum requirements of American National Standard for Information Sciences—Permanence of Paper for Printed Library Materials, ANSI/NISO Z39.48-1992.
Manufactured in the United States of America.

Contents

~

Preface

Fantasy Literature for Children and Young Adults is the culmination of many years of research, teaching, and a long-standing fascination with and love of this expansive genre we call fantasy. As authors, we are avid readers and, in particular, share a love of reading fantasy. As researchers, we each have been deeply interested in the various historical and critical approaches to evaluating fantasy literature and have spent many hours discussing the nuances, strengths, and of course weaknesses of hundreds of texts.

A key factor in the creation of this book, however, relates to our job as teachers. With a combined teaching experience of nearly eighty years, our work with young people and literature has provided us with a wealth of knowledge in all aspects of teaching and learning. One important belief we share is our commitment to finding ways to help our students become critical readers, writers, viewers, and thinkers as they acquire the habits of lifelong learning. We also believe that one way to do this is through the travels of the literature experience. While we have taught children's and young adult fantasy literature in our public school classrooms and university courses for many years, we have garnered our knowledge of the field through prolific reading of primary texts themselves, supported by critical reviews of the field in general. In teaching preservice teacher education students about the genre, we have continued to develop criteria that would help our students learn to evaluate the literature that they read and will ultimately teach in their own classrooms. This book, then, contains the insights we have gained through our own reading and research and a collection of the many evaluative techniques we have used in our own classrooms. Finally, it attempts to provide a resource for teachers—preservice and veteran—to develop a deeper understanding of the history of fantasy literature and the criteria used to evaluate it.

We thank our families for their support and encouragement of this multiyear endeavor; this fantasy is now a reality.

CHAPTER ONE

~

Introduction

Fantasy—what does it bring to mind? Undoubtedly, for many it raises images of witches, fairies, dark woods, magic wands and spells, time travel, ghosts, and dragons. Readers define fantasy in a personal way, depending on their own life stories, experiences, hopes, dreams, and fears. In creating this text, we have come together as students, teachers, and lovers of fantasy to share our personal understandings of this genre and to celebrate the universal messages that connect us as readers and storytellers across generations. This book is intended to help teachers and students of literature for children and young adults to develop their own understandings of this broad genre in order to evaluate and promote the joy of fantasy in their classrooms.

Throughout our professional journeys, we have focused our studies on literature for children and young adults and the teaching of reading in and out of classrooms. Just as sharing stories with others adds to a reader's understanding, so ours has gained by weaving together our three views. We hope that this expanded discussion of fantasy, together with the added layers that you bring to it, will result in an even broader understanding and serve as a springboard for further discussion. To that end, we offer a working definition, recognizing that it is also shaped by our own personal experiences. Springing from the depths of mythology and the Greek *phantasía* (making visible), fantasy literature represents our personal need and the universal quest for deeper realities and eternal truth. Fantasy is imaginative fiction that allows us to explore major life mysteries without being limited by size, time, or space. More specifically, fantasy literature, like all other forms of myth, springs from the human need to understand the struggle of good versus evil. All of ancient mythology reflects the give and take of this struggle; we still make and use myth, through fantasy literature, in order to deal with it. Herein lies the power of fantasy and myth, because the struggle never ends.

In this book we advance the premise that, as Bernice Cullinan suggests, "children who never read fanciful stories have a difficult time considering the possibility of fantasy. They are bound to the literal, the practical, the ordinary" (279). She further suggests, as do Bruno Bettelheim and Joseph Campbell, that fantasy and myth enable us to more easily imagine things better than or different from what we see in front of us. Fantasy and myth nurture the imagination that fuels our creative impulses. Without that ability to "make visible" something that does not exist, we would be limited indeed.

The Psychology of Fantasy

Fantasy may refer to the end result of the mental process of fantasizing, in which case it is a by-product of the mind's capacity to create images of objects not physically present or even possible. These images can be multiple or single, sequential or random. Fantasy may also be the content of daydreaming and reverie, the relatively harmless, short-lived kinds of fantasizing many people indulge in to help relieve boredom or pass the time. Or fantasy may involve the systematic assembling of imaginary personalities or the adoption of roles that enables some individuals to evade, if only for a while, a reality they perceive as indifferent or hostile. It is true that these meanings of fantasy belong more to psychology than to literature, yet literary fantasy is closely related to all the psychological processes just mentioned. Not only is the creation of literary fantasy often prompted by dreaming or reverie, but at a very early stage in the creative process it also actively involves mental images of objects not physically present or possible. Speaking of the composing of *The Lion, the Witch, and the Wardrobe*, C. S. Lewis remarked that it "all began with a picture of a Faun carrying an umbrella and parcels in a snowy wood"; curious about this picture, which he had been carrying about in his mind since he was sixteen, he had to go on, shaping a story that would provide context and point to the image (Lewis, "It All Began with a Picture . . . ," 53).

Indeed, it is no exaggeration to state that to be human is to fantasize. Yet not everyone agrees as to the appropriate place and value of fantasy in human life. On one side are those who charge that persons who day-dream frequently spend their time in unhealthy self-aggrandizement and that people fond of reverie merely indulge in useless nostalgia. More-over, the charge continues, fantasy may encourage some individuals to refuse to confront or resolve daily and long-term problems and tensions that mature people are expected to deal with. Therefore, these critics suggest, fantasy is evasive, escapist, and counterproductive; in fact, they conclude, it is a kind of moral and psychological cowardice. On the op-posing side are those who, while conceding that fantasy may facilitate evading problems or postponing their solutions, argue that the value of fantasy, or fantasizing, involves more than providing respite, however welcome and necessary, from the burdens of living or coping. The escape that fantasy makes possible, the argument goes on, is healthy and pro-ductive because, among other things, it can foster skill in designing sce-narios whereby individuals can pursue alternatives or try out new roles without actual risk. Hence, these advocates propose, fantasy needs to be cultivated rather than denigrated.

Ursula Le Guin dramatizes the debate in *The Beginning Place*, a novel ostensibly about heroism and quests but concerned too with the proper and improper uses of fantasy. Having found entry into the twilight coun-try, Tembreabrezi, where she has been able to come and go for over five years, Irene has made friends, learned some of the language, and fallen in love with the Master, Don Sark. However, she has never felt at home there, despite preferring the twilight country to an unhappy relationship with her mother, stepfather, and old friends. Increasingly, Irene senses within herself stagnation and frustration, the last because she cannot help her new friends, who are experiencing fear from some unknown source. Irene also finds it increasingly difficult to gain entry into Tem-breabrezi. A second protagonist, Hugh, while literally running away from an ineffectual, suffocating life—in particular a whining and nagging mother—bursts into the twilight country. There revitalized, he undergoes a rejuvenation that climaxes in his killing, with the help of Irene, a dragon-like creature terrorizing the land. As a result, both young people are able to escape their pasts and begin new lives. It becomes evident, as the story unfolds, that Irene, failing to perceive that the twilight country's true function is to be a beginning place for understanding and reordering one's life, has tried to use Tembreabrezi as an "ending" place where she can both evade problems and try to compensate for the evasion. On the other hand, from the start Hugh finds Tembreabrezi a genuine beginning place, feeling there the stirrings of new possibilities and different options that enable him to meet and overcome a life-threatening challenge and, hence, bring purpose and promise to his life.

The History of Fantasy

The direct ancestors of today's literary fantasy are traditional folk and fairy tales, which in turn can be traced to the myth-making of the classical oral traditions. The first literary fantasies for children and young adults appear in the nineteenth century with the publications of works by Hans Christian Andersen and Lewis Carroll's *Alice in Wonderland*. Although these works were heavily influenced by traditional tales collected by Charles Perrault, the Brothers Grimm, and others, they departed from the cultural renditions by removing some of the levels of didacticism. Both Andersen and Carroll incorporated the here and now into their stories, creating believable worlds filled with enchantment. This creation of worlds of enchantment is what sets literary fantasy apart from the cultural tales of the past. Literary fantasy, then, became a medium to sustain our need for heroes and our perpetual belief that good can overcome evil but without the level of moralizing found in earlier tales.

The Difficulty in Defining Fantasy

Any discussion of fantasy can involve misunderstanding, confusion, and paradox. As a consequence, anyone attempting an overview of fantasy

literature for children faces two distinct choices. One is to attempt to label and prune all the psychological, lexographic, and aesthetic thickets
surrounding fantasy, striving valiantly to distinguish elements common
to all the various understandings and uses of the term and hopefully
emerging triumphant, having in hand a universally acceptable theory or
definition of fantasy. The second choice is to accept and appreciate the
body of knowledge already accessible and employ whatever theory,
analysis, and criticism is available to serve the discussion. We have chosen the second option. From this point on, the word *fantasy* will refer to
a specific literary genre. Definitions and criteria proposed are intended
to apply primarily to children's and young adult fantasy; works and passages cited to illustrate or clarify will be taken as often as possible from
these works. Classifications, because they are descriptive and not pre-
scriptive, are designed to be tentative and flexible, accommodating any
new fiction and open to overlapping. Accordingly, individual works may
be discussed under more than one heading. Finally, because emphasis is
on children's and young adult fantasy literature, picture books, although
heavily dependent on the visual for their success, are included.

Qualities and Elements of Fantasy

Although literary fantasy or, to be precise, the fantasy written for children and young adults is the focus of this text, we remind readers that
fantasy exists in other art forms too: music, dance, theater, the graphic
arts, painting, and sculpture. One result of the various embodiments of
fantasy is that some critics and aestheticians, intrigued and challenged
rather than intimidated by what others suspect is the essence of fantasy,
strive to isolate its essential qualities and devise a universally valid definition. Yet this task is not easy; the path to its completion is strewn
with paradox, if not outright contradiction. Although there is a
plethora of possibilities, we offer the following six qualities as examples.

1. Because it often depends on images of what actually once existed
   or still exist, fantasy can be imitative and derivative.
2. Fantasy can be original and creative, as it selects bits and pieces
   of what once was or is, assembling them into new forms that have
   never existed.

3. Fantasy can be considered a conservative force, since its power to re-create what no longer exists or is not readily at hand insures retrieval, memory, and preservation.

4. Fantasy can also be an effective agency for change, renewal, and liberation when, refusing to be bound to the present and past, the visible and physical, and the traditional and established, it plays with what might be, makes what does not yet exist, and elaborates any number of possible futures.

5. Because of its unwillingness to accept restriction to the physical and finite, fantasy can dare aspire to the ideal, the transcendent, the luminous, and in so doing becomes a means whereby religion may be fostered.

6. Because of its penchant for outrageous what-ifs and its refusal to respect tradition and its trappings, fantasy can be subversive, ripping away facades, undermining the pillars of orthodoxy, and exposing the special pleading and self-interest often lurking behind convention and respectability.

Whether seen as aesthetic, social, political, or religious, fantasy, put as objectively and simply as possible, is imaginative fiction that can provide alternative realities, allowing us to explore issues of size, time, and space steeped in the human need to understand good versus evil. Additionally, for it to be considered as fantasy, two requirements must exist in children's and young adult literature.

1. Talking dogs, cats, mice, and pigs; sand fairies or, for that matter, fairies of any kind; objects that inexplicably transport people through time or over great distances; stuffed animals and toys, wind-up and otherwise, that can talk and walk; talismans that when rubbed or commanded grant wishes; potions that enlarge or shrink whoever drinks them; human beings normal in all respects except for being miniature or gigantic in size—all are examples of phenomena that do not and cannot exist in the world as it is physically constituted. The presence of one of these or any other "unreal" phenomenon in a work of fiction, regardless of how life-like or plausible every other element in that fiction may be, makes it fantasy.

2. At least one character in the work should be explicitly rendered as human or human-like so that readers, identifying with him, her, or it, care about what happens to that character. So strong is the reader's need to identify and empathize that, regardless of how richly detailed and evocative it may be, an imaginary world invites boredom and eventual rejection unless a human or sufficiently human-like character is also present with which readers, especially young ones, can become involved.

Two other criteria are often cited as essential to fantasy because they are salient features of especially admired or popular fantasies. First is an "arresting strangeness," the capacity of a fantasy to startle readers because it contains the strikingly different, the horrible, the awesome, or the bizarre. Second is some kind of internal order or rationalization; an effective fantasy, regardless of what physical law or principle of human behavior it violates or undermines, should operate consistently according to some such order or rationalization. However, these elements or characteristics are not universally accepted and may be more usefully understood as evaluative criteria.

Categories of Fantasy

Various types of children's fantasy have developed over the years. Historians, critics, and bibliographers of children's literature do not agree on the number of types that can be distinguished. For instance, Ruth Lynn lists in the first edition of her *Fantasy for Children: Annotated Checklist* thirteen types, one of which contains twenty-three subtypes (85). Moreover, specialists in the field are unable to agree as to what category of fantasy a particular book might belong. In an examination of the various ways specialists in the field have organized their discussions, we have chosen to limit the primary classifications to three: fairy or folk tales, mixed fantasy (which includes journey, transformation, talking animal, and magic), and heroic-ethical fantasy. Even when limiting primary categories to broad classifications, it is often difficult to place a particular work within a single category or subcategory. For instance, is L'Engle's *A Wrinkle in Time* mixed fantasy, heroic-ethical fantasy, or science fiction? Does Hoban's *The Mouse and His Child* belong to journey, transformation, or magic fantasy? Acknowledging that labeling of any texts can be difficult and limiting, we believe that if subject matter, plot, and intent are accepted as relatively objective indicators, a handful of helpful categories can be useful. Although each category is examined in some detail in later chapters, a brief description here may be helpful.

Fairy tales encompass two subcategories—folk fairy tales and court or art fairy tales. Folk fairy tales—for example, those collected by the Grimm Brothers and Joseph Jacob—supposedly mirror the lives and aspirations of the folk or common people and have their roots in oral tradition. On the other hand, court or art fairy tales are modeled upon folk fairy tales, sometimes even including material from them, but are deliberately crafted by an individual often for a courtly audience. These can be brief, like Charles Perrault's "Puss and Boots" and "Sleeping Beauty" and Hans Christian Andersen's "The Tinder Box" and "Great Claus and Little Claus," or lengthy, even novel length, like George MacDonald's *The Princess and Curdie*.

Combining realism and fantasy, mixed fantasy is of several types. Journey fantasy covers travel in both space and time, such as journeys from one place to another, from one time period to another; the adventures of a journey are an important element in this type. In transformation fantasy, the main character or characters undergo some kind of basic change, such as from inanimate to animate, from toy to real, from human to dragon. Talking animal fantasy concerns animals gifted with speech. Within magic fantasy exists a catchall subcategory involving power of mysterious origin. In this subcategory, the power impinges magically upon characters and their lives or is operative within one or more characters who either use it or learn how to use it.

The final category is heroic-ethical fantasy. Featuring heroic adventures and deeds, this category often involves the protagonist arriving at moral decisions that may have unexpected and far-reaching consequences.

Distinctions between Fantasy for Children and Adults

Because children's and young adult fantasy differs little from adult fantasy, any book for children or young adults is fantasy if at least one element in it cannot exist in the world as we know it. For instance, Arriety Clock and her parents in Mary Norton's *The Borrowers* are no different from any other working-class British family except that they are only a few inches tall. The remainder of the Clock family's physical appearance, the cut of their clothes, the furnishings of their residence, and their lifestyle and values are identical to those of normal-sized Britishers, once allowance is made for their physical smallness and the adjustment required to accommodate to a world geared for "gigantic" human beings. Moreover, any children's fantasy, by virtue of its being a children's book, invariably meets the second requirement for fantasy. That is to say, because the fantasy is first of all a children's book, it must already have a child protagonist, an adult character, or a human-like protagonist—a talking animal, a toy come alive, some imaginary creature—with which a child can readily identify.

Children's and young adult fantasy, therefore, can use any technique that adult fantasy uses. For example, the openings of two disparate fantasies, E. B. White's *Stuart Little* and Franz Kafka's *The Metamorphosis*, are similar in several important ways. White's story begins:

> When Mrs. Frederick C. Little's second son arrived, everybody noticed that he was not much bigger than a mouse. The truth of the matter was, the baby looked very much like a mouse in every way. He was only about two inches high; and he had a mouse's sharp nose, a mouse's tail, a mouse's whiskers, and the pleasant, shy manner of a mouse. Before he was many days old he was not only looking like a mouse but acting like one, too—wearing a gray hat and carrying a small cane. (chapter 1)

Almost immediately but not shockingly, Mrs. Little's expected-to-be-human son is transformed into a mouse, and in a matter-of-fact voice the author goes on to point out that, in spite of how "very unusual" it may be "for an American family to have a mouse," the Little family was delighted to have a mouse-son. Readers are not encouraged to speculate about how Stuart happened to turn up in Mrs. Little's womb.

Just as sudden an instance of transformation and just as matter-of-fact in its tone (which asserts that the bizarre change is not figurative) is found in the opening of Kafka's famous novella, *The Metamorphosis*:

> As Gregory Sams awoke one morning from uneasy dreams he found himself transformed in his bed into a gigantic insect. He was lying on his

hard, as it were armor-plated, back and when he lifted his head a little he could see his dome-like brown belly divided into stiff arched segments on top of which the bed quilt could hardly keep in position and was about to slide off completely.

Because the intentions of White and Kafka differ, the effects of the opening passages also differ; still, the technique—bizarre transformation, rapid narration, and matter-of-fact tone—is the same.

The Criteria for Successful Fantasy

Successful fantasy incorporates the following criteria: internal consistency, originality, a capacity to incite wonder, vivid setting, and style.

Internal Consistency

The fantasist (writer of fantasy) has the prerogative to create any number of ingenious happenings that flout the laws of nature and principles of human behavior. Although a fantasist can and does create imaginary worlds, beings, and happenings, readers have a right, perhaps even an obligation, to insist that what has been imagined or contrived should be explained and operate according to some law or principle, even if it is one devised by the author. For instance, if readers are told that a special coin can magically grant wishes (but only halfway), as they are informed in Edward Eager's *Half Magic*, then all subsequent permutations of plot and characterization must abide by that condition. Since Eager does this, the results in the story are zany and humorous. For instance, a girl, only physically half-present in a theater she wished to attend, is taken for a ghost and causes a near riot; or a woman, absentmindedly wishing she would be home, is whisked only halfway there and is dumped on a dusty country lane.

Another example of internal consistency can be found in another Eager book, *Seven Day Magic*, where the protagonists sit around discussing the laws governing magic, which they have learned from their wide reading of children's fantasy. One child protagonist insists, "The best kind of magic book . . . is the kind where the magic has rules. And you have to deal with it and thwart it before it thwarts you. Only sometimes you forget and get thwarted" (chapter 1).

A final example for the need of internal consistency can be found in a very interesting passage from Penelope Farmer's A *Castle of Bone*. Hugh, sensing that some law explains the workings of a magic cupboard, experiments by putting into the cupboard one button after another, hoping to discover how the cupboard returns various items to their pristine shape or nature. Failing in his experiment, Hugh longs "for one aspect of the cupboard to be controllable" (chapter 9).

Serious violations of internal consistency, whether deliberate or not, can result in narrative ambiguity. Oddly, Kenneth Grahame's *The Wind in the Willows*, a universally esteemed masterpiece of fantasy, contains several glaring examples of internal inconsistency. Sometimes Grahame depicts Toad as "toad-sized" and everything around him appears to be in proper relationship; other times, Toad seems very enlarged, his new size physically not fitting the circumstances in which he finds himself. For instance, when Toad gets behind the wheel, is his motor car "toad-sized" yet somehow large enough to drive safely down the road without being smashed by oncoming human-sized vehicles? On the one hand, if Toad's car is human-sized, having a normal-sized toad driving it strains credulity. In contrast, when White gives Stuart Little his own auto to drive with a cautionary reference to full-size road hazards, it has been downsized to accommodate the diminutive hero. When Toad, imprisoned and hoping to escape, thinks the gaoler's daughter is romantically smitten with him, is he toad-sized or human-sized? Grahame provides no explanation for these discrepancies, although it must have been his intent to have the animal's puffed-up physical size serve as a reflection of Toad's absurdly vain behavior. Incidentally, that Grahame's inconsistency did not prevent *The Wind in the Willows* from becoming a classic may be explained on either historical grounds—Grahame wrote before the importance of internal consistency was fully appreciated—or artistic grounds, that works of genius make and abide by their own rules.

Occasionally, what appears to be a violation of internal consistency is really not. Despite the apparent chaos that may trouble young, unsophisticated, or sensitive readers, Lewis Carroll's *Alice in Wonderland* is actually a marvel of internal consistency. Underneath the surface chaos operates a law of reversal of expectations: Whatever occurs belowground is the opposite of what Alice expects to find aboveground. For instance, in Wonderland, infants are pinched and made to cry instead of being petted and fondled; baby boys turn into pigs instead of staying human; and Alice, when she nibbles and drinks, drastically shrinks and stretches instead of growing normally. Once Alice realizes what basic law governs Wonderland, she can regain control of herself and her circumstances, and the dream comes to a close.

Internal consistency also refers to the author's handling of crossovers or transitions. In many fantasies, there is movement from the real world to a fantastic one, or a boundary is drawn between the two worlds, or a point exists where some fantastic phenomenon impinges upon reality. Barriers between the two worlds should be clear, and crossovers or penetrations justified. In *The Voyage of the Dawn Treader*, for instance, C. S. Lewis deftly handles the transition from Earth to Narnia. Edmund, Lucy, and Eustace are gazing at a picture of a Narnian ship at sea when, as both ship and sea suddenly become lifelike, the children smell salt water, feel sea breezes, and find themselves standing on the deck of King Caspian's ship. Although no reason is explicitly offered, Lewis implies—and the hint is explanation enough—that the children have been summoned to Narnia, where they are needed again. In *Charlotte's Web*, until Fern enters puberty and loses childhood's willingness to believe and trust uncritically, she can overhear the barnyard animals conversing among themselves, but she cannot speak to them or vice versa. Throughout the narrative, White carefully respects the barrier he created. In *Fog Magic*, Julia Sauer also makes puberty a barrier, this time between the past and the present. Until she turns twelve and begins the passage to adulthood, Greta is able to walk through the fog down the Old Road and visit the extinct village of Blue Cove.

Originality

Insisting on originality is justified even though the many new fantasies being published each year make it increasingly difficult for writers to achieve this goal. With so many entertaining fantasies already in print, one more talking animal or stuffed-toy-come-alive tale, quest novel, or story about a young person's becoming caught up in a struggle between good and evil can hardly be expected in itself to entice and retain readers. But work that is markedly original and fresh in subject matter, characters, setting, theme, or style stands a good chance of attracting readers' interest and attention. One unexpected result of insisting on originality is that, while the less talented or merely clever writer may be frightened away, resourceful and imaginative ones are challenged. As a consequence, original fantasies continue to be written. For instance, in *The Diamond in the Window*, the first of her richly allusive Concord fantasies involving the Hall family, Jane Langton both explores the relevance of Emersonian transcendentalism to contemporary life and counters the popular notion that fame and history are best utilized to lure tourists and their money. In *The Return of the Twelves*, a delightfully original tale about twelve wooden soldiers come to life, Pauline Clark fashioned a story based on the biographies of the Brontë children. Discovering that wooden toy soldiers were among the favored playthings of the famous siblings, Clark creates adventures for her toy soldiers as they march to the safety and security of a museum dedicated to Brontë memorabilia. Yet another example of originality appears in *Quag Keep*, where Andre Norton incorporates the popular fantasy board game Dungeons and Dragons into the plot. Additionally, Lloyd Alexander, Ursula Le Guin, and Mary Steele, employing plots as diverse as an assistant pig-keeper's seeking adventure and the chance to become a Hero (Alexander's *The Book of Three*), a talented youth's enrolling in a college for wizards and craving mastery over his peers (Le Guin's *A Wizard of Earthsea*), and a boy's setting out to discover the origin of the raft people floating on an underground river (Steele's *Journey Outside*), have dramatized in fresh, distinctive ways the theme of coming of age.

Paradoxically, insisting on originality brings about a renewed appreciation of the value of literary invention and tradition. A very skilled practitioner of fantasy as well as an astute critic, Lloyd Alexander has called attention to the appropriate stance a writer should adopt vis-à-vis traditional and conventional elements in fantasy. To clarify his point, Alexander uses the image of a story pot, a soup-like mixture of story elements into which writers can dip.

> Among the most nourishing bits and pieces we can scoop out of the pot
> are whole assortments of characters, events, and situations that occur
> again and again in one form or another throughout much of the world's

mythology; heroes and villains, fairy godmothers and wicked stepmoth-
ers, princesses and pig-keepers, prisoners and rescuers; ordeals and temptations, the quest for the magical object, the set of tasks to be accom-
plished. And a whole arsenal of cognominal swords, enchanted weapons;
a wardrobe of cloaks of invisibility, seven league boots; a whole zoo of
dragons, helpful animals, birds, and fish. ("High Fantasy," 579)

Alexander remarks that writers are welcome, subject to two conditions,
to dip into the pot and take out whatever strikes their fancy or meets
their needs. The first condition is that whatever is scooped out of the
pot of story should be used as skillfully as possible. The second, more
important condition is that writers who dip into the pot are asked to re-
plenish the story broth by dropping into it their own stories. This new
broth, then, becomes a skilled blend of the new and the old.

Thus, the making of successful fantasy calls for a mélange of original
and traditional, unfamiliar and familiar, unconventional and conventional, fresh and imitative. An important implication of Alexander's
remarks is that, since it is a blend of new and old, fantasy can surprise
and challenge readers while at the same time reassuring and comfort-
ing them. What is original in a fantasy may surprise, unsettle, and occasionally even shock young readers; as a result, they may become receptive to the challenges of confronting and accepting the unfamiliar
and new. On the other hand, the borrowed elements in fantasy—the
old, familiar, expected, and tried—provide young readers the desired
and needed security of meeting again what they previously experienced, as well as the keenly anticipated satisfaction of recognizing what
they already know. In other words, the conventional and traditional in
fantasy are anticipated and welcomed as familiar, reliable acquain-
tances, if not outright friends.

The Capacity to Incite Wonder

The single most important criterion for a successful fantasy is *the capacity to incite wonder*. This quality is essential to the work since without the element of wonder it fails as a fantasy. Wonder may exist in
three basic forms. First is the wonder or awe felt upon encountering the
strikingly different, the amazing, the bizarre, the alien, the Other. Second is the wonder or delight experienced when the cloud of routine, fa-

miliarity, ennui, and cynicism of our daily lives has lifted and we suddenly see with fresh eyes the beauty that was hidden. The third is the wonder brought about by the rekindling of faith in the existence of good and of hope in its eventual victory over evil. The second and third kinds of wonder involve recovery: reviving a moribund capacity to perceive beauty in the common and ordinary or enhancing this capacity if it is already active.

Fantasy may incite wonder through explicit statement and description, observed in *The River at Green Knowe* when Lucy Boston urges upon readers, first, the magic of moonlight and then the awe of Green Knowe:

> At its first coming the moon seemed almost to bounce up[,] its movement could be watched. But once properly in the sky, it hung like time. The children were so much under its spell that anything that might happen in its wild and ancient light could only seem in keeping. They were afraid only of missing the magic moment when the moon should sit [throming] on the point of their bedroom roof. . . . Green Knowe seemed smaller, but at the same time charged with awe. It has changed its friendly old fairy-tale quality for something far older and terrifyingly different. The house drew and held their attention, so that the transformation of the moonlight-fattened garden went unnoticed. ("Dr. Biggins Finds a Giant's Tooth")

Fantasy also may incite wonder through indirection, dramatic rendering, or displacement, the last a technique whereby something is shifted out of its customary setting and placed in a strange or novel one so that its worth may be perceived anew. For instance, in *A Wrinkle in Time*, Madeleine L'Engle demonstrates the power of love when Meg Murry, through her simple but courageous avowing of love for her father and younger brother, not only saves them from the evil *it* but also repels the black cloud threatening to envelop Earth. In the scene from *The Tombs of Atuan* depicting Ged's initial intrusion underground, Ursula Le Guin describes his clothing as permeated with the fresh, earthy, and fecund odor of the aboveground and outdoors. Le Guin both underscores the suffocating, barren existence of Arha, the young priestess "being eaten" by the dark forces of the underworld, and unexpectedly jars readers, reminding them of the elemental and vital power of soil, air, and sunshine.

Likewise, J. R. R. Tolkien insists in *The Hobbit* upon the basic human virtues of loyalty, commitment, and friendship. Tolkien embodies them not where they might be expected, in a human being, but surprisingly, in the apparently feckless and pleasure-loving hobbit and nonhuman, Bilbo.

Vivid Setting

In effective fantasy, a distinct sense of place is often crucial. Sometimes, a setting is so vividly described that it creates an atmosphere compelling readers to feel that magic is manifest or imminent—a sense that almost anything can happen. One thinks, for instance, of the moonlight-bathed river and banks in Grahame's *The Wind in the Willows*, which frame the animals' witnessing a divine epiphany, or the glistening estuary of the silver Dyfi River in Susan Cooper's *Silver on the Tree*, which recedes, revealing to Bran and Will the Lost Land and its city, which the boys enter on their quest for the crystal sword Eirias. Other times, a real place is described with such concrete and accurate detail that it acts as ballast or an anchor to reality, making the suspension of disbelief in the fantastic that much easier to achieve. Alison Uttley's *A Traveler in Time* describes the sights, sounds, and smells of the kitchen, farmhouse, and herb garden of the Thackers, which revitalizes the sickly Penelope Cameron and magically enables her to experience the life of Thackers back in the Elizabethan age. Richard Adams's *Watership Down* gives us Nuthanger Farm and its neighboring downs, where the rabbits' struggle for food, shelter, and survival and their fondness for story and myth become believable and catching. Finally, Penelope Lively's *A Stitch in Time* visits Lyme Regis, a seaside resort still emanating Victorian ambience, in which one house with its garden and swing gradually sensitizes Maria, the protagonist, to the presence of Harriet, who lived there a century earlier.

In many fantasies, the action takes place in imaginary or, as they have come to be called, secondary worlds. Because credibility of setting is essential to the success of these fantasies, knowledgeable authors strive to provide ample description of their secondary worlds and explanations of the laws governing them; in some instances, maps of the imaginary worlds are even devised. Obviously, the novelty and vivid detailing of the imaginary world, along with the clarity of its rationalization, can contribute to a fantasy's originality and capacity to incite wonder. The originality and credibility of its setting undoubtedly earned Laurence Yep's *Sweetwater* its Newbery Honor Medal. Surely before he began to write, Yep knew how his secondary world, Harmony, looked and was structured; hence, he was able to show clearly the interdependence of people and water there. Moreover, the climaxes of the novel—the swarming of the Sunfish into the streets of New Sion and the Silkies' valiant attempts to defend themselves from the Hudra—are exciting and plausible because of the extensive geographical and ecological exposition Yep had made earlier in the novel.

Style

What often makes for routine fantasy is the absence of a felicitous style, an absence especially damaging to fantasy's capacity to incite wonder. It is quite possible that the reason specialists in children's literature had neglected the L. Frank Baum's Oz books for many years stems from his unexciting style, which partially blinded critics to the other merits of the books and led them to lump the Oz stories with more pedestrian series fiction. Today Baum's fertile inventiveness—his broad array of fascinating characters, multiplicity of incidents, comic situations, evocative names, and diverse techniques for magically transforming ordinary objects into extraordinary ones—is cited, but virtually no one praises his style as distinctive. For instance, in *The Wonderful Wizard of Oz*, Baum blandly describes the room assigned Dorothy in the Palace of the Emerald City:

> It was the sweetest little room in the world, with a soft, comfortable bed that had sheets of green silk and a green velvet counterpane. There was a tiny fountain in the middle of the room, that shot a spray of green perfume into the air, to fall back into a beautifully carved green marble basin. Beautiful green flowers stood in the windows, and there was a shelf with a row of little green books. (chapter 11)

Contrast Baum's matter-of-fact description with Lucy Boston's evocation of a magic-filled moonlit night in *The Children of Green Knowe*:

> All the birds in the spruce tree woke up and flew out of the window, circling round St. Christopher with excited calls. The stone giant strode

across the lawns with his bare feet and soon came to the river. At the edge there was thin, loose ice that shivered like a window-pane as he stepped in. The water rushed round his legs and the reflection of the moon was torn to wet ribbons. The stream crept up to his waist and, as he still went on, to his armpits. When it looked as if he could go no farther Linnet heard a child's voice singing gaily. The sound was torn and scattered by the wind as the moon's reflection had been by the water, but she recognized the song as it came in snatches. ("Linnet's Story")

The magic of Green Knowe is almost palpable, and the attentive reader wants to believe that the statue of St. Christopher does walk on the lawns of Green Knowe. Indeed, distinctive style—the precise selection of words and phrases, use of metaphor and other figures of speech, euphonious arrangement of words, and alternating patterns of sentence length and form—is often the preeminent mark of successful fantasy.

A good test for the five characteristics of fantasy is to look upon them as qualities a work must have if readers are to accept it. Granted, some readers of fantasy are predisposed to accept anything placed before them that purports to be fantasy, but many more readers, less tender-hearted and incredulous, need a reason to believe in a work initially and to keep on believing. In all probability, if they decide to believe, the reason will be the presence within the work of internal consistency, originality, capacity to enhance or awaken ways of seeing and experiencing wonder, a vivid, detailed setting, and sensitivity to the sounds, sense, and patterns of words.

Works Cited

Adams, Richard. *Watership Down*. New York: Macmillan, 1974.

Alexander, Lloyd. *The Book of Three*. New York: Holt, 1964.

Alexander, Lloyd. "High Fantasy and Heroic Romance." *Horn Book Magazine*, vol. 47 (December 1971), 577–584.

Andersen, Hans Christian. *Fairy Tales*. New York: Grossett & Dunlap, 1945.

Baum, L. Frank. *The Wonderful Wizard of Oz*. Chicago: Reilly & Lee, 1956.

Boston, Lucy. *The River at Green Knowe*. New York: Harcourt, 1959.

Carroll, Lewis [Charles Dodgson]. *Alice's Adventures Underground*. 1865.

Clark, Pauline. *The Return of the Twelves*. New York: Morrow, 1965.

Cooper, Susan. *Silver on the Tree*. New York: Atheneum, 1977.

Cullinan, Bernice. *Literature and the Child*. 2nd ed. New York: Harcourt Brace Jovanovich, 1989.

Eager, Edward. *Half Magic*. New York: Harcourt, 1954.

———. *Seven Day Magic*. New York: Harcourt, 1962.

Farmer, Penelope. *A Castle of Bone*. New York: Atheneum, 1972.

Graham, Kenneth. *The Wind in the Willows*. New York: Scribners, 1933.

Grimm, Jacob, and Wilhelm Grimm. *Grimms' Fairy Tales*. New York: Grossett & Dunlap, 1945.

Hoban, Russell. *The Mouse and His Child*. New York: Harper, 1967.

Kafka, Franz. *The Metamorphosis* (1915). Trans. Stanley Corngold. New York: Bantam, 1972.

Langton, Jane. *The Diamond in the Window*. New York: Harper, 1962.

L'Engle, Madeleine. *A Wrinkle in Time*. New York: Farrar, 1962.

Le Guin, Ursula. *A Wizard of Earthsea*. New York: Bantam, 1975.

———. *The Tombs of Atuan*. New York: Atheneum, 1971.

———. *The Beginning Place*. New York: Harper, 1980.

Lewis, C. S. "It All Began with a Picture . . ." In *On Stories and Other Essays on Literature*, ed. Walter Hooper. New York: Harcourt Brace Jovanovich, 1982.

———. *The Lion, the Witch, and the Wardrobe*. New York: Macmillan, 1951.

———. *The Voyage of the Dawn Treader*. New York: Macmillan, 1952.

Lively, Penelope. *A Stitch in Time*. New York: Dutton, 1976.

Lynn, Ruth Nadelman. *Fantasy for Children: An Annotated Checklist*. New York: R. R. Bowker, 1979.

MacDonald, George. *The Princess and Curdie*. New York: Macmillan, 1945.

Norton, Andre. *Quag Keep*. New York: Atheneum, 1978.

Norton, Mary. *The Borrowers*. New York: Harcourt, 1953.

Perrault, Charles. *Histories or Tales of Past Times*. New York: Garland, 1977.

Sauer, Julia. *Fog Magic*. New York: Viking, 1943.

Steele, Mary. *Journey Outside*. New York: Viking, 1969.

Tolkien, J. R. R. *Hobbitt*. New York: Houghton, 1966.

Uttley, Alison. *A Traveler in Time*. New York: Viking, 1940.

White, E. B. *Charlotte's Web*. New York: Harper, 1952.

———. *Stuart Little*. New York: Harper, 1945.

Yep, Laurence. *Sweetwater*. New York: Harper, 1973.

CHAPTER TWO

~

Fairy Tales

Children are supposed to enjoy fairy tales, and in fact they do. Many young people ask for fairy tales to be read aloud. They end up selecting them as favorite stories or books, especially when they appear in attractively designed, illustrated, and colored picture books. Characters from individual fairy tales, like Cinderella, Snow White, Hansel and Gretel, Jack the Giant Killer, and Sleeping Beauty, once they have been introduced to children, become friends to rely on as a dependable (if imaginary) source of affection and support. Further, once they have learned to read, many children read and reread favorite fairy tales. It is, then, no surprise that most people do acknowledge a special association between fairy tales and childhood.

Children and Fairy Tales

The special relationship that children have with fairy tales makes them not only entertaining but instructive, contributing to children's education and socialization. The most common way of explaining this benefit is to point out that, because they are highly imaginative, fairy tales cultivate young imaginations. They also permit children, by facilitating self-imaging and self-identification, to gain entry into their own emotions as well as others', thus enriching their emotional and psychological experiences. By introducing or reinforcing wonder, beauty, and mystery, fairy tales also widen mental horizons and, in doing so, are invaluable in preparing the groundwork for children to acquire literary taste and gain access to their literary heritage. Finally, fairy tales can be used efficaciously to teach without overt sermonizing.

Some adults would go even further, perceiving the special association between fairy tales and children as natural. Representing this viewpoint is F. André Favat who, building upon insights of Jean Piaget, argues that important correspondences exist between the world of fairy tales and childhood. Favat begins by calling attention to children's beliefs that, through a process of participation, beings or objects can be directly related to each other, even though there is no spatial contact or intelligible causal connection. For instance, a child one day throws small white stones into a pool and the next day sees newly emerged water lilies; the child thinks there must be a connection. Moreover, young children are animists, attributing both consciousness and motion to inanimate objects, although by eleven or twelve they are willing to restrict consciousness to animals. Hence, children readily believe that boots can travel several leagues at a step, a prick to a finger can induce a ten-year sleep, and a horse's head or drops of blood can speak. Because of their interactions with parents and other adults, children take for granted their own lowly status. They are unaware of shifting, complex motives or actions and their implications. Through observation, they are convinced that simple, retributive justice is right. Small children have no trouble accepting the morality of fairy tales, which is often one of constraint, taboos, and physical control by individuals with the power to sanction by commands and prohibitions. Hence, the half-sisters of Cinderella merit punishment because they are mean and spiteful; and in the Grimms' "The Twelve Dancing Princesses" the many princes who fail to solve the mystery of the worn-out dancing slippers deserve to have their heads chopped off because that is the rule, and they knew it. Further, since young children respect authority, they accept that disobedience not only leads to trouble but goes against the "laws" of the world.

The final correspondences Favat claims between the world of fairy tales and childhood involve causality and egocentrism. Causality, why something happens, is not essential for the small child. What is important, however, are the actual events and their sequence—the what and how. Favat reminds grown-ups that the "and then . . . and then . . . and then" phraseology children use to tell their tales does not denote temporal, causal, or logical relationships but instead represents the personal connection events have for children as they spring to mind and are inserted into their stories. The absence, then, of strict causality in a fairy tale does not bother young readers, and to them a sponge, tied under a chin and hidden under a long beard—a device employed in "The Twelve Dancing Princesses"—is as good as any other container in which to pour a drugged wine. Finally, children are egocentric, sensing that the world revolves around them and that everything is either an extension of their feelings and desires or, at the very least, personally colored by a sense of themselves and their concerns. Accordingly, in fairy tales, that nature should cooperate with the protagonist—roses bloom in the snow, birds converse and advise, and briar hedges open up to permit entry—is proper. For what else is to be expected in a world which, as children see it, revolves around the protagonist and his or her concerns? Given the correspondences he finds between childhood and fairy tales, Favat concludes that fairy tales do embody "an accurate representation of the child's conception of the world" (38).

If the correspondences Favat describes actually exist, then it follows that as early as possible children and fairy tales should be brought together, and failure to do so means that some children will miss out on a kind of entertainment not readily available elsewhere. In truth, the loss may be even more serious inasmuch as children, by not being exposed to fairy tales, may be denied an opportunity to undergo storying—a process whereby the mind fundamentally structures and makes sense out of reality as it impinges upon the individual consciousness—which is essential to healthy maturation. Max Lüthi, discussing the impact that one fairy tale, "The White Snake," and by extension all fairy tales, can have on youth, contends:

> It is only the real world that has an effect on us; the story-book world, with its invisible images, is absorbed by our mind more easily and imperceptibly; this world is preformed and predestined to enter the treasury of our imagination and thus to take part in the building of our world. (67)

A few commentators, going still further, insist that fairy tales play an essential role in the healthy development of children. Perhaps the best known is Bruno Bettelheim, who in his controversial *The Uses of Enchantment* has argued for what he calls the right uses of fairy tales in the lives of children. Bettelheim's thesis is succinct:

> . . . fairy tales have unequaled value, because they offer new dimensions to the child's imagination which would be impossible for him to discover as truly on his own. Even more important, the form and structure of fairy tales suggest images to the child by which he can structure his daydreams and with them give better direction to his life. (7)

In the first part of the book, Bettelheim elaborates his thesis according to orthodox Freudianism, while in the second part he analyzes over twenty fairy tales to indicate how they can be employed to clarify children's problems. He is at pains to demonstrate that the imagery and form of fairy tales depict the two essential steps of growing up and "achieving" independence. The first step concerns finding an answer to the question of who the child is, and the answer, Bettelheim claims, is the same one psychoanalysis proposes: the integration of human ambivalences that unsettle and may even destroy. Although he admits that this integration is a life-long process, he suggests that in fairy tales it is presented as an accomplishment.

> [E]ach tale projects at its "happy" ending the integration of some inner conflict. Since there are innumerable fairy tales, each having some different form of a basic conflict for its topic, in their combination these stories demonstrate that in life we encounter many conflicts which we must master, each at its time. (90)

The second step involves a resolution of Oedipal conflict. Before children can be truly themselves, they must be free both of the power parents naturally have over them and of the power children give to parents "out of . . . anxiety and dependency needs, and from . . . [a] wish that they should forever belong only to them just as children feel they have belonged to their parents" (90). Bettelheim insists that the assistance that fairy tales give children in becoming integrated and free to be themselves takes place on the unconscious level; hence, adults can only speculate as to whether the assistance has actually occurred or may occur in a particular form. Further, this assistance is provided at the various stages of their development and, it must be stressed, in ways intelligible to them; also the kind of assistance is very dependent upon the experience and knowledge children actually have accumulated and the emotional preoccupations in which they may be embroiled. The aid fairy tales can give does not work magically or automatically; offered nonthreateningly with broad directionality (without specific solutions or directions), the aid may be accepted or rejected by children. Finally, since fairy tales utilize universal and often archetypal symbols, children can recognize and choose from among them. Therefore, the more fairy tales they are familiar with, the larger the repertoire of symbols and stories from which they can choose in order to construct their own stories and make sense of their own existence.

Strong objections have been raised to Bettelheim's approach to fairy tales and his individual analyses. Some fear that through his neo-Freudian eyes he finds far too much sexuality in fairy tales. Some believe his readings of individual tales are too mechanical or reductivist and breech their artistic integrity; some accuse him of being unscholarly and lacking historical perspective.[1] In fairness to Bettelheim, it must be kept in mind that he admits that his approach to fairy tales is definitely not the only one possible and can result in incomplete readings. In any case, it also should be noted that a good part of Bettelheim's defense of fairy tales is grounded in the fact that they are fantasy. It is quite possible, then, that the essential function of fairy tales that Bettelheim argues for can be attributed both to their distinctive format and to their being fantasy. In other words, the values of fairy tales—in particular, their broad directionality and their role in storying—are unique to fairy tales but may be discerned in other types of children's fantasy.

A close and special association between fairy tales and children has not been universally applauded or endorsed. There have always been those critics who believe that the enticing invitation to escapism, the physical violence, and the elaboration of violence and terror in word and illustration found in many fairy tales may have harmful or negative effects upon young minds and imaginations. In the absence of empirical data that demonstrate convincingly one way or the other, it is not

possible to allay completely these concerns or to ignore possible deleterious effects, especially upon very impressionable children. At the
same time, concerned adults should not underestimate the offsetting,
beneficent influence of the warm embrace and secure lap. The whole
affectionate, supportive environment that very often accompanies
fairy-tale telling is as much a part of the experience as the story itself.

There are also those who endorse fairy tales but only non-sexist
ones. Warning against the sexism they see pervading many tales, they
specifically point to the overwhelming masculine cast of society and
culture, the stress on feminine physical beauty, and the frequent plot
resolutions involving marriage whose "they lived happily ever after"
formulaic conclusion implies that now all important problems have
been forever solved. It is not enough, they also argue, that fairy tales
have female protagonists like Snow White, Cinderella, Sleeping
Beauty, Rapunzel, and Gretel—a phenomenon sometimes proposed as
proof that, of all forms of traditional children's literature, fairy tales are
least sexist and therefore commendable. Too many of these female protagonists, it is charged, are presented as passive, reacting women rather
than ones who can take charge of their own destinies.[2]

This contemporary uneasiness over the close relationship between
fairy tales and childhood is nothing new. It is simply the most recent
version of an antipathy to fairy tales exhibited by earlier generations.
For example, in late eighteenth- and early nineteenth-century Great
Britain, reformers, moralists, and educators such as Peter Parley
(Samuel Goodrich), Sarah Trimmer, Mary Sherwood, and Maria Edge-
wood, all sincerely concerned about what was best for the welfare of
souls, the training of young minds, and the developing of proper social
habits, were openly hostile to most fairy tales, claiming they were too
fanciful, escapist, and time-wasting. The only fairy tales recommended
were those carefully edited and made to promote proper and moral be-
haviors. Interestingly, Jack Zipes has suggested that another reason for
the hostility of these and similar reformers toward fairy tales was the
suspicion that the latter, still capable of having a potentially strong impact upon the lower classes (historically the prime source and audience
for fairy tales) might encourage attitudes and values antithetical to the
bourgeois values for which these reformers stood.[3] In other words, what
troubled them was not that fairy tales stimulated unbridled imagination

so much as it was their fear of the unrest and dissatisfaction that might follow if unbridled imagination took a political course.

Further study is needed to determine the validity of Zipes's explanation and similar ones that attribute to social and political causes the acceleration of interest in fairy tales during the eighteenth and nineteenth centuries in Europe (in particular, Germany and France, the first countries whose fairy tales were collected). However, the more recent research into the origin, development, and use of fairy tales makes clear that whatever explanation scholars ultimately agree on will include political, social, psychological, and cultural factors. One undisputed point is that fairy tales originally and for several centuries subsequently were primarily an adult literature—this despite persistent assumptions by many grown-ups that they exist only to entertain children. Only in the last two centuries has an association between childhood and fairy tales been developed and increasingly deemed important.

The Nature of Fairy Tales

Generally speaking, fairy tales are short narratives composed or written in prose. Common to virtually all fairy tales is also a prosaic quality, including a blend of clarity, terseness, and down-to-earthiness. This, combined with little ornamentation and a fondness for repetition and generic, abstract description (e.g., an old man, an old hag, the youngest son, the oldest princess) lends to fairy tales their distinctive sound, look, and style. Part of the distinctive style is a highly oral quality which, given their origins, is understandable. Fairy tales not only sound as if they are being recited but often contain elements that hint at the presence of a speaker who addresses the story to an audience that likes to be entertained and appreciates good story-telling technique.[4]

Stressing action, fairy tales expend relatively little time and energy in setting up scenes, describing locale, and portraying characters. Eschewing detailed descriptions of all kinds and often omitting proper names, fairy tales focus on essentials. Hence, such details as are provided, like the cloth on which there are three drops of blood or the soldier's long beard, are not filler but contribute significantly to the action: The loss of the cloth in the Grimms' "The Goose Girl" subjects the true princess to the false maid's power, and the beard in "The

Twelve Dancing Princesses" is long enough to hide a sponge into which the old soldier can pour the sleep-inducing wine that the eldest princess offers. That fairy tales do not render consciousness or analyze behavior and motives does not mean that human feelings and relationships are neglected; instead, they are addressed or commented on indirectly through objective plot elements, to whose implications, it must be presumed, audiences are open. For instance, in "Rapunzel" the mutual affection of the couple can be inferred from the husband's willingness to risk discovery and possible punishment as he steals into the neighboring witch's garden to find the salad herb (*Rapunzel*, the German for lamb's lettuce, or rampion; the Italian is *ramponzolo*) that his pregnant wife craves.

Fairy tales do not delineate the history and destiny of individuals as distinctive personalities; rather, one senses that individual characters, even if their names have become popular, represent types or tendencies in human nature or strategies for survival. Moreover, Max Lüthi wryly has remarked that in fairy tales individual characters never seem to be able to figure out how an action that led to unforeseen difficulties may, when repeated, bring about the same outcome. The capacity of characters to learn or their failure to do so, and the reasons for a character's finding luck or being denied it—in short, the mysteries of human behavior—are not the concerns of fairy-tale tellers or listeners; what is, is what happens next. At the same time, because fairy tales are full of melodrama, the affairs of their chief characters—who are usually depicted as extremes, good or bad, strong or weak, wise or foolish—veer abruptly from misfortune to even greater misfortune and then, just in time, turn to good fortune.

The well-known introductory formula "once upon a time" aptly indicates that the fairy tale's disregard for detailed characterization extends also to locale and strict chronology; as has been noted by many, the world of fairy tales is "place-less" and "time-less." Yet, paradoxically, events within this world reflect the same concern for weighty matters, such as survival, rebirth, growth, and maturation that the commonly experienced, pragmatic space-time universe has, and they also assume an idealistic world where Edenic harmony will exist by the end of the story among humanity, animals, and nature. Interestingly, commentators as early as the Brothers Grimm have pointed to the prominence in fairy tales of helping or grateful animals, a prominence that may signify that individuals possess powers that need nurturing before they can unfold or intensify. On the other hand, it may represent nothing more than the conviction or hope of speaker and listeners that humanity, animals, and nature are indeed interdependent. Within the world of fairy tales, too, miracles (the result of divine intervention in the affairs of human beings) and magic are not the object of surprise or admiration. Their appearances are a matter of course; their existence is so much taken for granted that miracles and magic must be acknowledged as pervasive in fairy tales. Further, it can be argued that, irrespective of the beliefs of listeners or story tellers, miracle (which presupposes divinity) and luck (which does not) function similarly as far as the requirements of plot are concerned. For example, in "The Twelve Dancing Princesses," an old soldier walking down a road meets an old hag and, as luck or providence would have it, helps her; out of gratitude, she shares with him the secret of the twelve princesses and their worn-out dancing shoes. Doing as he had been directed by the hag, the soldier solves a mystery and is rewarded a princess for a wife and part of a kingdom for a dowry. Whether it is good luck or a miracle, as far as plot outcome matters, is immaterial.

Protagonists in fairy tales come from all social classes and are of both sexes. Generally speaking, they enjoy similar fortunes: Having fallen from a relatively high social status to a lower one or already being situated there when the tale begins, the protagonists by its end either are returned to their high status or are substantially elevated. The rags-to-riches feature of fairy tales, along with the prominence of miracles and luck as the means by which protagonists achieve success, strongly suggests that the origin of fairy tales and their historical capacity to sustain interest owe much to individual or group wish-fulfillment on the part of listeners. That is, since the one group of listeners most inclined to engage in wish-fulfillment of this magnitude is the peasant or the commoner, the rags-to-riches pattern points to the origin of fairy tales among the folk or common people.

Two important features of fairy tales remain. One is that the protagonists are frequently challenged explicitly to meet goals or fulfill purposes that involve journeys taken, physical ordeals undergone, or some kind of testing endured. Often obstacles block the quest or restrict the

purpose, and these must be overcome or circumvented. The other feature is the prevalence of the number three: three sons or daughters,
three tasks, three obstacles, three helpers, three wishes, and so on.
While some people believe the fondness for three in fairy tales reflects
the mystery and power associated with the Christian belief in the trin-
ity, others suggest the prevalence of three needs no explanation other
than that it is part of the abstract style characteristic of fairy tales.
These features stand out in "The Devil's Three Golden Hairs." The
evil-hearted king attempts three times to have the good-luck child dis-
posed of by drowning, by murder, and by seeking three golden hairs
from the devil. Three times the youth evades death: through luck (the
coffin-like box does not sink), through luck and coincidence (he loses
his way and is befriended by robbers who have a change of heart), and
through wile (he connives with the devil's grandmother). At the end,
he is triumphant and the king punished.

Virtually all commentators attribute the longevity of fairy tales to
the fact that they are art and, as such, symbolic of fundamental human
concerns and interests. This consensus, however, dissolves when specific and detailed interpretations of the symbolic in fairy tales are proposed. One school of thought considers some fairy tales remnants of ancient nature and religious myths. Accordingly, the good witches or
fairies invited to the christening of the new princess in the variants of
"Sleeping Beauty" represent the months of the solar cycle, while the
malevolent witch or fairy stands for the discarded lunar cycle. Or Little
Red Riding Hood's cape is red because that color, along with the girl's
being swallowed by and then freed from a wolf, echoes an ancient solar
myth. Another school argues that the old fairy tales express primitive
beliefs and practice. Hence, the prominence of red, the sign of blood,
in the "Red Riding Hood" tale points back to a primitive belief that
women menstruating are taboo to men except for any who are "wolfish"
sexual predators. In "The Goose Girl," for another example, the importance of the cloth with three drops of blood, which the queen
mother gives to her daughter and enjoins her not to lose, reflects the
medieval insistence upon the physical virginity of the bride so that her
father-in-law, seeing the blood-spotted sheets the morning after the
wedding night, might rest easy and not fret over possible illegitimate
heirs. A third school, grounded in psychoanalysis and dream interpre-

tation, sees in fairy tales evidence of fundamental human tensions, struggles, and drives. According to this view, the real basis of the Snow White story is incest, a father's fear that he is fated to have a sexual encounter with his daughter. Or, an alternative reading proposes, the impetus for Snow White's tale is the older step-queen's fear that she may be losing her physical beauty and whatever power she wields because of it, and her desire to eliminate all potential rivals, especially a younger and very beautiful step-daughter.[5]

These various interpretations, it should be realized, are suppositions and tentative readings and by no means proven or established. At the same time, regardless of what one may think of them, the interpretations help in appreciating the multilayered richness of fairy tales and in perceiving that certain beloved or popular stories may have been preserved for centuries not by accident but by previous generations' sensing their relevance. The interpretations and the approaches to understanding fairy tales that they illustrate should not be dismissed out of hand on the grounds that they are highly unsuitable for children. Fairy tales, it should always be kept in mind, did not originate and develop just for young people. Fairy tales do resonate with meaning, and adults are understandably intrigued to explore this meaning; moreover, the exploration can be carried out without subscribing to any one particular school or approach. Perhaps the soundest advice to anyone pondering symbolic or "hidden" meanings in fairy tales is that he or she should become aware of the various readings and interpretations, adopt a "both . . . and" strategy instead of an "either . . . or" one, and constantly remain open to new findings and insights.

Types of Fairy Tales

Fairy tales are conveniently divided into two categories, folk and art. Folk fairy tales tend to be old, some of them (or, to be precise, parts of them) being traceable to the dawn of recorded history. They are an oral literature, created by storytellers and told to audiences who, there is reason to believe, were active collaborators in the shaping of the tales. These tales were passed on from one generation to another by storytellers who very likely retained, added, or embellished the tales to fit their audiences' needs and preferences. The term "folk" indicates the debt these tales have to the folk or ordinary people—the peasants, the lower classes. Although the exact nature of this debt is open to dispute, in general it suggests that the attitudes, values, aspirations, and needs of the common people are both reflected and articulated in folk fairy tales. The tellers of folk fairy tales were of course anonymous, and only in the eighteenth and nineteenth centuries, when the tales first began to be collected (most notably by the Brothers Grimm), did information about the storytellers and their remarkable feats of memorization and narration become available. The Grimm brothers' collection of folk fairy tales may be the most famous and arguably the most influential of all collections, but by the end of the nineteenth century virtually every European country and others throughout the world had their folk fairy tales systematically collected and edited, out of the conviction that these tales, because they constituted an important part of a people's cultural and historical heritage, required preservation.

The origin of folk fairy tales is unsettled. Some experts champion monogenesis—the theory that a particular tale originated in one place and then, as people came to like it and wanted to share their enjoyment with others, spread gradually over a large area. Other experts, however, contend that polygenesis is a more likely explanation; because they represent universal situations or natural relationships, similar tales originated in different lands at different times as the people needed to express, articulate, or find value in a particular concern or situation. Regardless of which explanation is ultimately vindicated, it is a fact that similar versions of tales exist in many countries. For example, according to one recent count, seven hundred variants of the Cinderella story have been collected (Opie, 121). In addition, folklorists have discovered that, when a folk fairy tale is analyzed, various story elements or motifs can be isolated and shown to appear in tales from around the world.

The phenomenon of recurrent motifs has deepened understanding of the universality of folk fairy tales and their structure. In his book *Morphology of the Folktale*, V. Propp has argued that, at least in European fairy tales, some of the more significant motifs—such as those describing the functions of the hero, his family, and his antagonists—are limited in number and appear only in a certain sequence. Although an individual fairy tale need not incorporate every hero motif, those the tale does contain will follow the expected sequence.

Understanding the origin of fairy tales is complicated by the possibility that folklorists may need to discard the previously accepted view that a sharp demarcation exists between folk and art fairy tales. It has been customary to believe, for example, that Charles Perrault incorporated elements of folk fairy tales into his tales, and speculation centered on where he might first have heard the stories from which he borrowed elements and which he then embellished for his own amusement or the court's. Supposedly, a line of influence ran from the common people to the author, the court, and a slowly emerging middle class, all of whom for one reason or another came to find the old people's tales amusing. However, there is now evidence that some of the tales told at court—art fairy tales, in other words—somehow may have been made available to the general populace (or returned to the people, for all anyone really knows) and subsequently found their way into the storyteller's repertoire and became accepted by the people as their own (Calvino, xxiv–xxv). The possibility that a supposed demarcation between folktales and art fairy tales is no longer valid reminds us that, in discussing fairy tales, making generalizations is risky, since most of them will be shown to be incomplete, undocumented, or just plain incorrect.

Art fairy tales are deliberately crafted by individual, known artists who either incorporate elements actually borrowed from folk fairy tales or imitate their form and spirit. Although often having an oral quality, art fairy tales are primarily literary, composed to be read as well as heard. As for their being preserved for subsequent generations, the survival chances of art fairy tales depend, as in the instances of other literary works, upon the talent of their creators and the degree to which they successfully incorporate or imitate fairy-tale form. Accordingly, while *The Troubles of Queen Silver-Bell* and *The Spring Cleaning*, those arch and lifeless imitations by Frances Hodgson Burnett, are virtually forgotten, the vibrant and sensitive tales of Oscar Wilde are still read. In Wilde's "The Selfish Giant," for instance, the scenes of children's seeking entrance into the Giant's garden and playing and hanging in branches, dangling like fruit, and the Giant's being embraced by a child are still memorable. Wilde poignantly fuses magic and the Christian insight that love and redemption can be earned through suffering.

Because art fairy tales are composed by individual authors, often they have a distinctive flavor reflecting those writers. The famous French compiler and adapter of fairy tales, Charles Perrault, who is responsible for the first published appearance of "Little Red Riding-Hood," "Puss in Boots," and "Bluebeard," gives his tales a sophistication and elegance one expects from a courtier of the seventeenth-century French court. A similar kind of sophistication and elegance can be found in the stories of Madame d'Aulnoy and Madame Leprince de Beaumont, probably the two most talented of the seventeenth-century noblewomen who made names for themselves by composing fairy tales. Perhaps the most well-known writer of art fairy tales, Hans Christian Andersen, definitely has placed upon his work the stamp of his personality and imagination. On one hand, an Andersen tale like "The Little Match Girl" or "The Steadfast Tin Soldier" reflects controlled pathos and the ability to give endearing vitality to common, everyday objects. On the other hand, tales like "The Ugly Duckling" or "The Red Shoes," with their barely submerged envy and self-pity, exude Andersen's own suffering and personal unhappiness.

Art fairy tales are often much longer than folk fairy tales, sometimes novel-length, and yet they retain most of the essential characteristics of the latter: a matter-of-fact acceptance of magic and miracle; a tendency to type and to extremes in characterization; a close relationship between characters and nature; emphasis upon action rather than introspection and description; a relatively clear style; and the presence of goals, quests, and obstacles, both internal and external. However, if there is any one distinct difference between folk and art fairy tales, it is the latter's capacity to suggest to readers that their meaning is multilayered; literal reading, although interesting and even exciting, does not exhaust their significance. Interestingly, in Victorian England the long art fairy tale became quite fashionable; consider for example, William Thackeray's *The Rose and the Ring,* John Ruskin's *The King of the Golden River,* Tom Hood's *Petsetilla's Posy,* Maggie Browne's *Wanted: A King,* or Mark Lemon's *The Enchanted Doll and Tinykin's Transformations.* Surely the most important and successful of these authors composing novel-length art fairy tales is George MacDonald, whose novels were instrumental in sustaining the Victorians' fondness for long fantasy and today are still read for enjoyment and recognized as pioneering myth-based fantasy.

Probably the best written and structured of George MacDonald's long fairy tales is *The Princess and the Goblin*, the story of a miner's son, Curdie, who comes to the assistance of Princess Irene when she is kidnapped by the goblins. Although he has no assigned quest as such, Curdie has his tasks—to save the Princess from the goblins and, before he can accomplish that, to prove his worth by demonstrating, after initial failure, an ability to see Queen Irene, the very old Dowager Queen, whose youthful loveliness is visible only to those who have faith in the existence of goodness and its capacity to overcome evil. The major characters are distinctive: Curdie and his parents, commoners and salt of the earth; the Dowager Queen, the King, and Princess Irene, royalty (the last two of whom learn that nobility of rank is not identical to moral nobility); and the ugly and evil goblins who dwell below the mountains. The Grandmother is the most interesting character, since her function is to be the children's fairy godmother, whose magic and inspiration are available only to those who can perceive perennial youth under the exterior of an old woman.

Other typical features of the fairy tale are present in *The Princess and the Goblin*: a formulaic opening, a quasi-oral quality, medieval setting, a protagonist of low status, reliance on poetic justice, and the requisite happy ending. Moreover, the narrative is more than just a long and simple fairy tale. Both Curdie and Irene, through the agency of Queen Irene, the archetypal matriarch and the moral center of the narrative, undergo psychological growth as well as spiritual regeneration. More importantly, boy, girl, and old-young woman and what befalls them represent MacDonald's attempt to show that goodness really is strong and good people are genuinely likable and even fun to be with, and not priggish, stuffy, boring, and ineffectual.

Art fairy tales continue to be written. James Thurber's whimsical *Many Moons* is both fairy tale and commentary on how the magic of fairy tales works, a magic that enables the Jester successfully to adjust the requirements of a factual truth to those of the Princess's emotional well-being. Randall Jarrell's *The Animal Family*, with its fairy-tale features of abstract characterization, the use of three, reliance on magic, presumption of sympathy between nature and human, and simplicity of style disguising tenderness and profound insight, celebrates bonding and family. Very early in his popular and beloved *The Little Prince*, Saint-Exupéry remarks:

> I should have liked to begin this story in the fashion of the fairy-tales. I should have liked to say: "Once upon a time there was a little prince who lived on a planet that was scarcely any bigger than himself, and who had need of sheep . . ."
>
> To those who understand life, that would have given a much greater air of truth to my story. (section iv)

The form of a fairy tale may not be evident in *The Little Prince*, but to most who read it the "truth" of fairy tales is manifest.

Picture Books and Fairy Tales

Picture books often provide a sound alternative for discovering various readings and interpretations of fairy tales. By exploring the many and varied versions of fairy tales through the illustrations as well as the text, we can find hidden meanings, subplots, and cultural attitudes. Criteria used to evaluate picture books can be found in any number of books about children's literature. The one incorporated for our purposes here, however, is a composite of many and suggests that we evaluate picture books on the basis of the artful use of visual representations, language, and specific use within the genre of fantasy. Furthermore, the criteria demand that the visual representations and illustrations capture and hold the reader's interest while amplifying or extending the text; that the language have an internal storytelling rhythm that is intrinsic to the unfolding drama; and that elements of the story—characters, setting, plot, theme, style, and mood—be consistent with the genre of fantasy, and in this instance, fairy tales or folktales.

Renditions of fairy tales and folktales abound within picture books. Although Marian Roalfe Cox reports on a remarkable number of versions of Cinderella in her book *Cinderella: Three Hundred and Forty-Five Variants*, it seems that one can find nearly as many illustrated versions in local bookstores and libraries. Such variants as *Yeh-Shen*, retold by Ai-Ling Louie and illustrated by Ed Young; *The Egyptian Cinderella*, by Shirley Climo and illustrated by Ruth Heller; *The Rough-Face Girl*, by Rafe Martin and illustrated by David Shannon; or *Moss*

Gown, by William Hooks and illustrated by Donald Carrick contrast sharply to Perrault's version, as retold and illustrated in *Cinderella* by Diane Goode. The classical French tale, rendered in watercolor and pen and ink, is full of light, airy depictions of men and women dressed in the French style of Louis XV, while *The Rough-Face Girl* and *Moss Gown* reflect dark, ominous settings of the forest and swamp. A significant cultural contrast also can be found in the illustrations for *Yeh-Shen*, in which Ed Young uses the ancient Chinese panel art to depict this variant dating back to the T'ang Dynasty (A.D. 618–907).

Another fairy tale that lends itself well to illustration is *Hansel and Gretel*. The various retellings depict a variety of interpretations of how the witch and her house of sweets might look. For instance, after the children are abandoned in the forest a second time by their father and his wife, they wander until they find a cottage made of bread, roofed with cakes (cookies or pancakes), with windows of sugar (clear sugar, barley sugar, or sugar candy). Although the description of the house construction is similar across texts, the various illustrations of the house itself range from less than appetizing—as found in Lisbeth Zwerger's rendition of a plain white cottage with roof tiles that resemble shake shingles or Adriene Adams's version of a cottage with mushroom-like shingles—to Lesser and Zelinsky's or Susan Jeffers's cottages of pancakes, wafer cookies, candy canes, gumdrops, and frosting. There is little doubt as to why the Hansel and Gretel of Lesser and Zelinsky's or Jeffers's retellings rushed to devour chunks of the delectable abode.

Another interesting detail in the adventure of Hansel and Gretel that differs greatly from one variant to the next is the depiction of the witch. As with the differences in cottages, the witches seem to range from cartoonish, to grotesque caricatures, to plump, wizened, old crones. Once again, it is the Lesser and Zelinsky and Jeffers versions that seem to entice the children rather than scare them away. The illustrations resonate significant differences in depictions of good and evil, enticement and trickery. Some versions are obvious in their implications of danger—an ugly witch, an ugly stepmother, as seen in the interpretations by Zweger or Adams. Others, however, such as Zelinsky and Jeffers, use the enticement of beauty and sweets to lure the children into coming closer to the hidden evils of the witch—a warning that still looms over all children about the danger of taking candy and sweets from strangers.

Finally, "Little Red Riding Hood" continues to be retold and illustrated in ways that inform and caution children about the evils of talking to strangers. Many versions, such as those by Tina Schart Hyman and James Marshall, have Red Riding Hood and her grandmother rescued by a woodcutter who kills the wolf and frees them from the belly of the animal. Another version, though, does not end as happily. Author and illustrator Christopher Coady chooses rich, dark jewel colors to represent the darkness and danger of the woods and wolf. This haunting rendition leaves the reader with a moral:

> From that day until this, the sad story of Red Riding Hood has been a lesson to all little children . . . meant to make them frightened of creatures like wolves who can be pleasant and charming when other people are nearby. But these creatures can be dangerous indeed, as Red Riding Hood unfortunately found out. (Coady, 27)

Ed Young chooses to begin his variant, *Lon Po Po: A Red Riding Hood Story from China*, with an acknowledgment: "To all the wolves of the world for lending their good name as a tangible symbol for our darkness" (1). This version also is filled with dark, ominous watercolors which, when placed into the Chinese panel art form, draw the reader into a world of fear and trickery. As with all the variants, the theme is one of caution and danger—to be fearful and distrustful of strangers.

These variants, along with hundreds of others, are art fairy tales—tales that are intended to be experienced through text and illustrations. The illustrations extend the text and provide support for the story elements of characterization, setting, plot, theme, style, and mood—elements in folktales that were once the work of the oral storyteller.

Retellings and Renditions of Fairy-Tale Novels

Fairy Tales Retold

Authors have retold fairy tales for centuries; the very nature of oral storytelling is based on the retelling of tales from one court to another, from one village to another. Recent decades have found the retelling of fairy tales of major interest for authors of young adult and mid-level fiction.

Three authors who have done much to bring fairy tales to older readers include Gail Carson Levine, Robin McKinley, and Donna Jo Napoli. All three authors have received prestigious awards for their works from the Newbery to the American Library Association best books lists. Levine captured the interests of young readers with her retelling of "Cinderella" in her Newbery award book, *Ella Enchanted*. With Ella's birth, a "gift" of obedience is placed upon her by a fairy. A gift of obedience is recognized as the curse it is, however, when it becomes evident that Ella must do whatever is commanded of her, forcing her to become a slave to those who would seek to control her—particularly those evil stepsisters. Ella's struggle to escape the curse takes her into a world of new challenges where she must discover who she really is and of what she is capable, showing readers that glass slippers and fancy balls do not a princess make.

Robin McKinley creates a new twist to the story of "Beauty and the Beast" in her first retelling of it, *Beauty*. While earlier fairy-tale versions describe Beauty as the only beautiful and kind daughter of the merchant father, McKinley's retelling places Beauty in a loving and supportive family where she is called upon to use her intelligence to cope with newly austere country life when her father faces financial ruin. When she is needed to step forward save her father's life by moving into the castle with the Beast, she accepts her duty and finds over time that trust and affection develop between herself and the Beast. While the ending stays true to the original tale, the character development of Beauty is cast as one of growth and maturation—situating it strongly as a coming-of-age novel.

Twenty years later McKinley again retells this favorite tale in *Rose Daughter*. McKinley gives Beauty the gift of caring for roses and in her effort to bring life to the dying rose gardens of the Beast, she finds life and love in the process. While McKinley again stays true to the plot structure of "Beauty and the Beast," this retelling is steeped in the elements of romance and rebirth and the importance of transformations in life.

In a third retelling of a fairy tale, McKinley takes the reader into the story of "Sleeping Beauty," in *Spindle's End*. Although the curse is duly cast, this story sends the young princess away to a village to live as a blacksmith's apprentice. McKinley weaves a tale that is rich in imagery and detail with an interesting twist to the traditional "happily ever after" ending.

Beginning with *The Prince of the Pond*, Donna Jo Napoli has created a series of books that put a modern twist on classic fairy tales. Told from the perspective of the main characters—often the presumed villain—Napoli manages to tell the other side of the story. *The Prince of the Pond* is both a retelling of a fairy tale and an animal fantasy. The main characters are the male and female frogs, but this time the male is a prince who has been turned into the amphibian by a hag. Discovered by the female frog, he is confused and nearly helpless until she educates him in the ways of the pond. Both are granted human speech, humor, and values as they attempt to adjust to a frog's life. Pin, as he is called, never quite gives up his human ways of doing things, and with a twist meets a somewhat bittersweet end. Though written for a younger audience, this work has potential as a read-aloud.

Better known and considered one of her best, *Magic Circle* demonstrates Napoli's talent. While remaining faithful to the original tale of Hansel and Gretel, *Magic Circle* is set in the medieval period and told from the point of view of the witch. This first-person narrator becomes a sympathetic heroine as we discover how she was a midwife and devoted mother before falling prey to the devil's tricks. Other retellings include *Spinners*, the story of Rumpelstiltskin, which she co-authored with Richard Tchen. Here Napoli employs yet another narrative approach, telling the story from the perspectives of the villain and later the miller's daughter who is really Rumpelstiltskin's daughter. In *Zel*, a retelling of *Rapunzel*, Napoli again demonstrates her craft. Multiple narrators tell the story, set in Switzerland during the Reformation. Chapter by chapter the characters take turns, sharing their stories and leaving their marks on the reader. Rapunzel, the mother, and Konrad are complex characters who share their hopes and fears, each becoming sympathetic and memorable. Significant themes of parental conflict, sexuality, love, betrayal, and loss are deftly handled in this ingenious novel.

Napoli continues to grapple with themes of real life in her retellings of fairy tales. Her most recent work, *Crazy Jack*, provides readers with a fresh look at the traditional tale of "Jack and the Beanstalk."

Fairy Tales Rendered Anew

Combining fantasy with realistic fiction is a recent trend in fairy tales for young adult readers. Such authors as Jane Yolen and Francesca Lia Block have provided mid-level readers with provocative renditions set in historical and realistic settings. In these stories, the fairy tale becomes the metaphor that serves as the context for the present-day plots. Yolen juxtaposes the tale of "Sleeping Beauty" with the horrid reality of the Holocaust. In contrast, Block's delightful modern-day fairy tale layers the often unbelievable world of Hollywood with the elements of the genre.

In *Briar Rose*, Jane Yolen retells the Holocaust tragedy, using the earliest known version of "Sleeping Beauty" to frame it. Rebecca Berlin promises her dying grandmother that she will uncover the identity of Briar Rose, the character of her favorite fairy tale. She is determined to discover whether or not her grandmother's claim to be Briar Rose is true. Becca, a journalist, travels to Poland with the essential three clues of her inheritance: a ring, a photograph, and the story of Briar Rose. She begins to search her grandmother's mysterious past. In her search, Becca learns how in life the thorn accompanies the flower and discovers much more than the answer to her question.

A popular novel by Francesca Lia Block, *Weetzie Bat*, is a delightful and clever modern day fairy tale for young adults. If, as Bernice Cullinan states, "folklore provides a way of seeing a different culture"(165), *Weetzie Bat* does indeed afford us a look into the very hip, out-of-the-ordinary life of a teenager in Los Angeles. Often described as a fairy-tale place itself, Los Angeles provides the backdrop for this charming and offbeat coming-of-age fairy tale.

Block crafted this novel to include virtually every archetype, convention, motif, and theme of the traditional fairy tale. The protagonist's quest is to discover for herself certain fundamental truths and achieve happiness. Along the way, she meets a genie in a bottle, a wicked witch, and a benevolent crone. She is granted three wishes, faces three crises, and in discovering meaning in her own life achieves happiness. Throughout, Weetzie exhibits cleverness, bravery, wisdom, kindness, and sensitivity.

The novel begins rather traditionally with the sentence, "The reason Weetzie Bat hated high school was because no one understood" (3).

But that is where the expected ends. Weetzie lives on her own. Her mother, Brandy-Lynn, is a starlet, and her father, Charlie Bat, is a screenwriter who has moved back to New York after their marriage broke up. Weetzie meets her best friend Dirk at school on the first day of the semester. She describes her immediate attraction. "Dirk was the best looking guy at school. He wore his hair in a shoe-polish-black Mohawk and he drove a red '55 Pontiac" (4). Dirk was instantly drawn to Weetzie as well. "She was a skinny girl with a bleach-blonde flat-top. Under her pink Harlequin sunglasses, strawberry lipstick, earrings dangling charms, and sugar-frosted eye shadow she was really almost beautiful" (4). Weetzie loves the life of L.A. with its plastic, Hollywood artifacts but also values kindness, people, and relationships.

Dirk has lived with his Grandma Fifi since his parents died, and together Dirk and Weetzie visit her whenever they need comfort. Grandma Fifi is a sweet, powdery old lady who bakes tiny, white, sugarcoated pastries for them, plays tunes on a music box with a little dancing monkey on top, has two canaries she sings to, and has hair Weetzie envies—perfect white hair that sometimes has lovely blue or pink tints. Grandma Fifi have Dirk and Weetzie bring her groceries, show her their new clothes, and answer the same questions over and over again. They feel very safe and close in Fifi's cottage (6–7). Grandma Fifi is the ultimate benevolent crone.

Dirk confesses to Weetzie that he is gay, but it doesn't matter to her because they are best friends. Both are looking for their perfect mates, living hard, fast lives but not having much luck connecting with anyone. Grandma Fifi recognizes their sadness and consoles them, assuring both that they would be happy in love some day. As a special gift, Fifi goes in the closet and returns with a gift for Weetzie, a dusty, gold urn.

Back home, as Weetzie begins to clean and polish it, a genie emerges in a cloud of musty vapor. "Weetzie could see him—it was a man, a little man in a turban, with a jewel in his nose, harem pants, and curly-toed slippers" (23). The man promptly announces, "I am the genie of the lamp, and I am here to grant you three wishes" (23). Weetzie answers, "I wish for a Duck (or mate) for Dirk, and a Secret Agent Lover Man for me, and a beautiful little house for us to live in happily ever after" (24).

Almost immediately they hear that Grandma Fifi has died and left them her cottage, "a Hollywood cottage with one of those fairy-tale roofs that look like someone had spilled silly sand" (26). Next, Dirk finds a lover, Duck, but still Weetzie is alone. When she wasn't expecting it, Weetzie meets My Secret Agent Lover Man in a coffee shop. He talks her into appearing in a film he's making, and they fall madly in love. The four of them, Dirk, Duck, Weetzie, and My Secret Agent Lover Man, move into Grandma Fifi's cottage and begin their lives happily ever after, although Weetzie begins to question what happily ever after means. Meanwhile the film is a success and they make some money and begin to reward themselves. "I feel like Cinderella," Weetzie comments (42).

Weetzie decides she would like to have a baby, but My Secret Agent Lover Man believes that the world is too much of a mess to bring a child into. When Weetzie gets pregnant by either Dirk or Duck, it is too much for My Secret Agent Lover Man, who leaves. Weetzie has a baby girl they name Cherokee and begins to raise her with Dirk and Duck.

After a time, My Secret Agent Lover Man returns to L.A., suffering from a curse put on him by Vixanne Wigg, a witch with whom he had a brief affair and who is now pregnant. His curse is lifted once he agrees to speak with Vixanne. Shortly thereafter, they find a basket on their doorstep containing a witch baby, along with Barbie and Ken voodoo dolls as a peace offering. They name this child Lily, but the name doesn't stick and she is known hereafter as Witch Baby.

Weetzie then goes into a deep depression when she hears the news that her father, Charlie Bat, has died of a drug overdose. And finally, upon finding out that his friend Bam Bam is dying of AIDS, Duck leaves, disillusioned. Dirk is determined to find him and manages to locate him in San Francisco and bring him home. At the end of the novel, they are all reunited around the table, reflecting on life and relishing their happiness. Weetzie philosophizes that "love and disease are both like electricity. They are always there . . . We can choose, Weetzie thought, We can choose to plug into the love current instead" (88).

The language of the novel captures the essence of the fairy tale. With its unusual names and colorful descriptions, the narrative begs to be read aloud, enjoying the use of repetition and word games. Expressions like

"Lanky Lizards," and names like Weetzie, Grandma Fifi, and My Secret Agent Lover Man capture the reader's attention. And who can resist the description of Weetzie and My Secret Agent Lover Man's first kiss?

> A kiss about apple pie a la mode with the vanilla creaminess melting in the pie heat. A kiss about chocolate, when you haven't eaten chocolate in a year. A kiss about palm trees speeding by, trailing pink clouds when you drive down the Strip sizzling with champagne. A kiss about spotlights fanning the sky and the swollen sea spilling tears all over your legs. (37–8)

Although the novel doesn't begin with the traditional "Once upon a time," the last line does close with a happy ending. "I don't know about happily ever after . . . but I know about happily, Weetzie Bat thought" (88).

This modern-day fairy tale challenges the reader to expand previously held perceptions about the genre. Although Block may appear to push the limits of acceptable social mores within her fairy-tale rendition, none can argue her fresh application of the form.

Finally, *Heckedy Peg* by Audrey Wood, illustrated by Don Wood, and *The Girl Who Loved the Wind* by Jane Yolen are two stories that effectively demonstrate that it is possible to re-create both the form and spirit of fairy tales so that they continue to delight and inspire. *Heckedy Peg*, for instance, is a story inspired by a sixteenth-century children's game that richly fulfills the criteria of artful use of visual representations and language specific to the genre of fantasy. Its illustrations capture the reader's interest and extend the text through a number of carefully designed uses of color, shape, and foreshadowing, while the language of the text is both rhythmic and dramatic. Instead of the usual "Once upon a time. . . ." beginning, Audrey Wood creates a parallel with "Down the dusty roads and far away. . . ." She continues the parallel with a description of the protagonist and her place in life: "a poor mother once lived with her seven children named Monday, Tuesday, Wednesday, Thursday, Friday, Saturday, and Sunday." To this text, Don Wood created a picturesque setting of home and hearth full of happy, smiling children working together, bathed in the richness of warm tones of gold, amber, red, and orange. The faces of the children are healthy and beautiful with eyes bright with a glint of mischief. As soon as readers turn the page, however, they are met with dark images of a concerned mother issuing a warning to her children as she leaves for the market: "Now be careful, and remember—don't let a stranger in and don't touch fire." Through the window, behind the children now at play, we can see the cause for the dark contrast in coloring and mood—a witch with a cart coming over the bridge toward the home of the now unchaperoned children.

Don Wood uses the richness of color and detail throughout to extend the rhythmic language of the text. After the children have let Heckedy Peg into their home and have given her the fire to light her pipe, she throws it to the floor, shouting "Now I've got you!" and turns them into food. Don Wood illustrates this wicked happening with visions of translucent children turning into solid samples of food. The expressions on the faces of the children represent shock and fear as they fade into what is meant to be supper for the witch. At the end of the story, when the good mother is able to solve the riddle and rescue her children from Heckedy Peg, Don Wood once again shows joy and happiness by a rush of bright, warm colors against the dark background of the witch's cottage. The mother and her children are bathed in golds and ambers while Heckedy Peg and her surroundings are dark and misshapen forms—contrasting good and evil in its basic levels.

Conclusions

The relationship between young people and fairy tales continues to be important to the development of and cultivation of young imaginations. By introducing or reinforcing wonder, beauty, and mystery, fairy tales also widen mental horizons and, in doing so, are invaluable in preparing the groundwork for children and young adults to acquire literary taste and gain access to their literary heritage. Finally, fairy tales can be used efficaciously to teach without overt sermonizing, allowing young people to discover the hidden dangers of the world (as well as the magic) through the experiences of strong characters, faraway settings, and interesting plots.

Notes

1. Typical of the attacks on Bettelheim's position is Robert Darnton's in "Peasant Tell Tales: The Meaning of Mother Goose," in *The Great Cat Massacre and Other Episodes in French Cultural History* (New York: Basic Books), pp. 10–13. A more sympathetic critique is James W. Heisig's "Bruno Bettelheim and the Fairy Tales," *Children's Literature* 6 (1977): 93–114.

2. A very useful collection of essays that summarizes the various objections to fairy tales, as well as discussing and arguing their merits today, is "Fairy Tales: Their Staying Power," *CHLA Quarterly* 7, no. 2 (Summer 1982): 1–36; see in particular Ruth MacDonald's "The Tale Retold: Feminist Fairy Tales," 18–20.

3. Patricia Miller, "The Importance of Being Earnest: The Fairy Tale in 19th-Century England," *CHLA Quarterly* 7, no. 2 (Summer 1982): 11–14. Zipes's study is *Breaking the Magic Spell: Radical Theories of Folk and Fairy Tales* (Austin: University of Texas Press, 1979).

4. Our discussion of the characteristics of fairy tales is indebted to Max Lüthi's balanced and perceptive study, *Once Upon a Time*; the approach and facts are his; their application to individual tales, ours.

5. Throughout his study, Lüthi discusses most of the anthropological and psychological interpretations. Another helpful discussion of the latter can be found in the introductions to the various tales collected in Iona and Peter Opie's *The Classic Fairy Tales* (London: Oxford University Press, 1974). A very recent, thorough application of myth to fairy tales is L. C. Cooper's *Fairy Tales: Allegories of the Inner Life* (Wellingborough, UK: The Aquarian Press, 1983).

Works Cited

Andersen, Hans Christian. "The Little Match Girl," "The Red Shoes," "The Steadfast Tin Soldier," and "The Ugly Duckling," in *Fairy Tales*. New York: Grossett & Dunlap, 1945.

Bettleheim, Bruno. *The Uses of Enchantment: The Meaning and Importance of Fairy Tales*. New York: Alfred Knopf, 1976.

Block, Francesca Lia. *Weetzie Bat*. New York: Harper Trophy, 1999.

Browne, Maggie. *Wanted: A King*. Illus. Harry Furniss. Verses by S. H. H. Duckworth & Co., 1910.

Burnett, Frances Hodgson. *The Spring Cleaning*. New York: Century, 1908.

———. *The Troubles of Queen Silver-Bell*. New York: Century, 1906.

Calvino, Italo, ed. *Italian Folktales*. New York: Pantheon Books, 1981.

Climo, Shirley. *The Egyptian Cinderella*. Illus. Ruth Heller. New York: Harper, 1989.

Coady, Christopher. *Red Riding Hood*. New York: Dutton, 1992.

Cox, Marian Roalfe. *Cinderella: Three Hundred and Forty-Five Variants of Cinderella, Catskin, and Cap O' Rushes, Abstracted and Tabulated, with a Discussion of Medieval Analogues and Notes*. London: London Folk-Lore Society, 1891; published with an introduction by Andrew Lang in 1893. Kraus Reprint, 1967.

De Saint-Exupéry, Antoine. *The Little Prince*. New York: Harcourt, 1943.

Favat, F. André. *Child and Tale: The Origins of Interest*. Urbana, Ill.: NCTE, 1977.

Goode, Diane. *Cinderella*. New York: Knopf, 1988.

Grimm, Jacob, and Wilhelm Grimm. "The Devil's Three Golden Hairs," "The Goose Girl," "Little Red Riding Hood," "Rapunzel," "Sleeping Beauty," "Snow White," and "The Twelve Dancing Princesses," in *Grimms' Fairy Tales*. New York: Grossett & Dunlap, 1945.

Hood, Tom. *Petsetilla's Posy*. NewYork: Garland, 1976.

Hooks, William. *Moss Gown*. Illus. Donald Carrick. New York: Clarion, 1987.

Hyman, Trina Schart. *Little Red Riding Hood*. New York: Holiday House, 1983.

Jarrell, Randall. *The Animal Family*. New York: Pantheon, 1965.

Jeffers, Susan. *Hansel and Gretel*. New York: Dutton, 1986.

Lemon, Mark. *The Enchanted Doll and Tinykin's Transformations*. New York: Garland, 1976.

Lesser, Rika. *Hansel and Gretel*. Illus. Paul O. Zelinsky. New York: Putnam, 1984.

Levine, Gail Carson. *Ella Enchanted*. New York: HarperCollins, 1998.

Louie, Ai-Ling. *Yeh-Shen*. Illus. Ed Young. New York: Philomel, 1982.

Lüthi, Max. *Once Upon a Time: On the Nature of Fairy Tales*. Bloomington, Ind.: Indiana University Press, 1976.

MacDonald, George. *The Princess and the Goblin*. New York: Macmillan, 1945.

Marshall, James. *Little Red Riding Hood*. New York: Dial, 1990.

Martin, Rafe. *The Rough-Face Girl*. Illus. David Shannon. New York: Putnam, 1992.

McKinley, Robin. *Beauty*. New York: Harper and Row, 1978.

———. *Rose Daughter*. New York: Greenwillow, 1997.

———. *Spindle's End*. New York: Penguin, 2000.

Napoli, Donna Jo. *Crazy Jack*. New York: Thorndike Press, 2003.

———. *Magic Circle*. New York: Penguin, 1995.

———. *Prince of the Pond*. New York: Penguin, 1994.

———. *Zel*. New York: Penguin, 1998.

Napoli, Donna Jo, and Richard Tchen. *Spinners*. New York: Penguin, 2001.

Opie, Iona and Peter. *The Classic Fairy Tales*. London: Oxford University Press, 1974.

Perrault, Charles. "The Blue Beard," "Little Red Riding-Hood," and "The Master Cat or Puss in Boots," in *Histories or Tales of Past Times*. New York: Garland, 1977.

Propp, V. *Morphology of the Folktale*, 2nd ed. Trans. Laurence Scott. Austin: University of Texas Press, 1968.

Ruskin, John. *The King of the Golden River*. New York: Greenwillow, 1978.

Thackeray, William. *The Rose and the Ring*. New York: Avon, 1965.

Thurber, James. *Many Moons*. New York: Harcourt, 1943.

Wilde, Oscar. *The Selfish Giant*. New York: Harvey, 1967.

Wood, Audrey. *Heckedy Peg*. Illus. Don Wood. New York: Harcourt Brace, 1987.

Yolen, Jane. *Briar Rose*. New York: Tom Doherty, 2002.

———. *The Girl Who Loved the Wind*. New York: Crowell, 1974.

Young, Ed. *Lon Po Po: A Red Riding Hood Story from China*. New York: Philomel, 1989.

Zwerger, Lisbeth. *Hansel and Gretel*. New York: Picture Book Studio, 1988.

CHAPTER THREE

~

Mixed Fantasy

The History of Mixed Fantasy

The most common type of children's fantasy is what we call mixed fantasy: children's fiction that combines fantasy and realism in various ways and proportions. The familiar subtypes of mixed fantasy include journeys (time travel), transformation, talking animals and toys, and magic. Mixed fantasy is so prevalent that observers may suspect that it has always been a part of children's literature. And in a way they are right, if *Alice in Wonderland,* a story about a girl who dreams she has fallen into an underworld where she enjoys many wondrous adventures, marks the definitive beginning of a genuinely imaginative literature for children. Regardless of its popularity and longevity, mixed fantasy presents for authors and readers alike special problems of plausibility because it mixes two seemingly incompatible universes. For example, E. B. White wants readers to take seriously a story joining what cannot exist—a talking pig and spider—with what can exist—a young farm girl who tries to save the runt of a litter. If the real and unreal universes are joined to form mixed fantasy, authors must meet particular conditions in order to create believable settings, characters, and conflicts. These conditions are best illustrated through a discussion of the work of Edith Nesbit—what has come to be known as the Nesbit Legacy.

The Nesbit Legacy

Edith Nesbit, a fine children's writer whose productive career spanned the nineteenth and twentieth centuries, is often credited with recognizing the need for establishing guidelines for the mixing of realism and fantasy, particularly in the areas of plot and coherence. These solutions subsequently have been adapted and refined by other writers of mixed fantasy. Admittedly, Nesbit was not the first children's author to wed the fantastic and real in a long narrative. For example, Lewis Carroll's several fantasies preceded Nesbit's, but despite their brilliance they spawned no successful imitations, and Carroll established no school or following. George MacDonald also combined fantasy and realism. In *At the Back of the North Wind*, remarkably imaginative passages in which the North Wind demonstrates and explains to Little Diamond why she inflicts pain and suffering upon people are intermingled with scenes of contemporary cabby life in London. Little Diamond is a "blessed" innocent, privileged to enjoy fantastic adventures through North Wind's power and favor; at the same time, the young boy, whose brain has been damaged by fever, is also the son of a London cabby living in realistic workingman's surroundings. But MacDonald remained essentially the creator of fairy tales. What Nesbit did, on the other hand, was to show that realism and fantasy can be mixed so consistently, entertainingly, and significantly that other authors, noting her success, followed her direction; eventually mixed fantasy became established as the dominant form of children's fantasy. The solution Nesbit devised to address the problems stemming from the blending of fantasy and realism can be examined in the Psammead trilogy, which depicts what happens when normal children are given access to and some control over a magic that unexpectedly and surprisingly impinges upon their lives.

The Children and It, the first segment of the trilogy, is a series of episodes, each complete in its own chapter, involving four children, Robert, Cyril, Anthea, and Jane, and their adventures with magic. Both children and setting are realistically described, and this portrayal, in addition to the realistic content and context of the various adventures, provides the book a kind of ballast, so that the fantastic framework of the adventures stands a very good chance of being accepted by readers. Although magic is the cause of the children's adventures, its agent is not the conventional fairy godmother but the Psammead, Nesbit's own creation, which is a querulous but somewhat likable mixture of snail, bat, spider, and monkey. In granting wishes, the Psammead follows its own pattern: first inhale, balloon, and then exhale; claiming exhaustion, it will grant only one wish a day. The Psammead, perhaps because it is so grouchy, grants wishes sometimes literally and quite loosely. It may give the children something they never really intended or expected, such as a frustrated wish that their baby brother be full grown or the acquisition of newly minted money that is rendered suspect because of its earlier coinage.

Gradually, the children learn to cope with the Psammead's magic and its rules, but in the process they occasionally overlook, with amusing results, the cardinal rule that the effects of magic cease at sunset. For instance, the children, having sprouted wings to fly, forget the sunset rule in their sky-frolicking and become stranded up on a church tower. What is significant in the scenes describing the children's coping is that, as the Psammead's magic operates, it seems domesticated, rationalized, and controlled. Nesbit's readers would hope to find these characteristics duplicated in their own wished-for adventures involving magic. The Psammead's magic does not operate by chance; as long as the children apply their intelligence and resourcefulness, it can be controlled. Chaos is not a result of magic; if it occurs, it is the children's fault.

The second volume, *The Phoenix and the Carpet*, pretty much repeats its predecessor in approach and technique; the only interesting difference is that the children travel farther afield for their adventures. But in the third volume, *The Story of the Amulet*, the best written and best thought-out of the trilogy, there is a noticeable change in Nesbit's handling of the interface of magic and reality. The narrative is definitely more complex than its predecessors. The structural dependence on one incident per chapter is dropped, and incidents develop over several chapters. New characters are added; the children's relationship with adults is broadened and deepened; a quest—to seek the missing half of a Babylonian amulet—provides order and point; and time travel backwards and forwards complements the simple wish-fulfillment and geographic traveling the children enjoyed in the previous volumes. Overall, the incidents are by far fresher and more interesting, provocative, and dramatic than those of the preceding stories. Nesbit's research is clearly evident in the description of the places the children visit. In particular, details of life in ancient Egypt, Babylon, Atlantis, and in a London of the future are accurate or intelligently speculative. The net effect of the structural and stylistic improvements is to give readers additional persuasive grounds for not just suspending disbelief in the fantastic but actively accepting it.

Nesbit's handling of magic is noteworthy. Initially, she expands the function of magic beyond merely granting the children's wishes or satisfying their lighthearted or frivolous desires. Magic can be serious; for instance, it helps the children understand the various foreign languages they hear during their travels. Hence, Robert, Cyril, Anthea, and Jane must be initiated into magic's many uses. It, too, has been provided a source—Babylonian and Egyptian astrology and cult practice, a "prescience," so to speak—that supposedly can tap into a power existing somewhere "out there." Finally, for the first time Nesbit acknowledges that magic can be wielded for evil purposes and not just mischievous, embarrassing, or awkward ones. As a result, plot and characterization in *The Story of the Amulet* are relatively somber. Interestingly, in using magic to account for the children's capacity to understand and speak foreign languages, Nesbit feels compelled to come up with some kind of rationalization for the children's being able to do something incredible. Occasionally, she seems a bit embarrassed by her weak explanation.

> Now, once for all, I am not going to be bothered to tell you how it was that the girl could understand Anthea and Anthea could understand the girl. You, at any rate, would not understand me, if I tried to explain it, any more than you can understand about time and space being only forms of thought. You may think what you like. (chapter 4)

The point is that Nesbit concedes the necessity for some kind of rationalization. The same necessity is also behind her rationale for the children's time travel; an amulet that expands when certain words are spoken is transformed into a portal through which the children can travel into the past and future.

In her very next novel, *The Enchanted Castle*, Nesbit consolidated the breakthrough of the Psammead trilogy. Again she employed four intelligent, well-read, sensitive, and resourceful children—Gerald,

Jimmy, and Kathleen, siblings, and their new friend, Mabel—and places them in a setting realistic in every respect except that magic is manifest. The four children, like those in the Psammead trilogy, are the kind who might experience magic because they believe in it and are ready to recognize it. These children also try to behave as normally as possible in the unexpected presence of magic and to master, if possible, its workings. As in the Psammead trilogy, much of the book's delight stems from observing the children as they learn to adapt to the sometimes dangerous power manifest in a magical ring——a power far more extensive than they first thought or imagined. For example, the ring can bring to life the Uglies-Wuglies, a group of bizarre "characters" that the children devise out of clothing and common household objects and plan to use for a family entertainment. In a nightmarish scene, before the troublesome Uglies-Wuglies are successfully tricked and shoved into a mausoleum that they think is a hotel, they become openly hostile and inflict bodily harm.

Nesbit continues in *The Enchanted Castle* to take magic very seriously, attributing to it an independent existence somewhere nearby but off Earth. This time she links magic and its operating principles with humanity's dream of a Golden Age. When these principles are superficially understood or carelessly wielded, magic can become a mere wishing ring, its effects taken for granted, such as when Mabel is invisible, a small statue of a dinosaur quickens into life, or Kathleen turns into a stone giant. When the full power of the ring is clarified, however, the children discover that there is a land independent of Earth where magic rules.

Occasionally, a mortal can pass through a gossamer curtain that separates the world of magic and the world that only seems real. Moreover, because of "little weak spots" in that curtain, a ring or an amulet for instance, incredible phenomena may occur. There is a special night, the fourteenth day when the moon rises, when all mortals are permitted to enter the land of magic. (The children, ever resourceful, puzzle this out when the night occurs.) On this night everyone—mortals, demigods, and gods represented by the statues in the castle's garden—can assemble to pay homage to an eternal light that sustains and gives meaning to the universe. In other words, for *The Enchanted Castle*, Nesbit created her own myth to explain the existence of magic and its operations.

Edith Nesbit's direct legacy is considerable. First, she laid the groundwork for the development of mixed fantasy through her pioneering use of multiple protagonists, strategies for eliminating the restrictive presence of parents, and situating protagonists in a social and cultural context conducive to adventure. Second, she demonstrated that the kind of fantasy she was writing is open to both humor and seriousness and that in it there need be no conflict between them. She was among the very first, if not the first, to employ children's fantasy to investigate the moral ambiguity of human behavior and intentions without oversimplification or undue complexity—an investigation subsequent fantasists have continued to pursue with great effect and success. Third and lastly, Nesbit insisted that mixed fantasy's audience is intelligent and perceptive; as such, it does not have to be preached at, although it is receptive to information and speculation, and definitely does not want to be patronized. Paradoxically, the high standards Nesbit set in insisting upon the intelligence of her readers and the respect due them may actually be a reason why today her books are not widely read or recognized as they deserve to be.

Virtually all practitioners of mixed fantasy have benefited from Nesbit's pioneering work, but there are some authors who have either consciously modeled their work upon her fiction or incorporated much of her spirit and posture into their own. Edward Eager illustrates the former, while Jane Langton, the latter. Openly acknowledging his fondness for Nesbit, Eager even depicts his young protagonists as hugely enjoying reading her fiction. In *Half Magic*, for instance, he says:

> This summer the children had found some books by a writer named E. Nesbit, surely the most wonderful books in the world. They read every one that the library had, right away, except a book called *The Enchanted Castle*, which had been out. And now yesterday *The Enchanted Castle* had come in, and they took it out, and Jane . . . read it out loud all the way home, and when they got home she went on reading, and when their mother came home they hardly said a word to her, and when dinner was served they didn't notice a thing they ate. (chapter 1)

In *Half Magic*, Jane, the eldest of four siblings, whose surname is never given, accidentally finds what she believes is a coin, which she soon discovers is actually a talisman that magically grants whatever one asks for while holding it. Jane also discovers to her dismay that the talisman grants only one-half of what is requested; consequently, she must be careful to ask for twice as much as what she actually wants. Each child uses the talisman to have one exciting adventure apiece: Mark, exploring the desert; Katherine, visiting King Arthur's court; Martha, attending the theatre; and Jane, becoming a prissy, spoiled child. The adventures do not always turn out the way the children expect. Intermingled with the children's adventures is a subplot involving a romance between their mother and Mr. Smith. All ends happily when the talisman's power allows the children and their mother to acquire their hearts' desire—remarriage and a warm, contented family life. The book concludes with another child finding the talisman and beginning to discover how it operates.

Clearly, *Half Magic* is mixed fantasy, in which everything is realistically rendered except for the existence of the talisman and its power and the adventures initiated by magic. A possible exception is the characters' attaining their hearts' desire, an outcome potentially attainable without the intervention of magic. Evidently having learned from Nesbit, his mentor, Eager carefully lays out the laws governing magic; the talisman intervenes in human affairs when most opportune and appears only to those children willing to believe in magic and hence capable of taking advantage of its manifestations. Since the four children must learn to abide by magic's laws, this learning process provides much of the book's humor and precipitates the various adventures that make up the plot. The magical talisman is both the rationale for the plot and the agent whereby the protagonists and, indirectly, the readers receive their "heart's content." Interestingly, the talisman temporarily loses its power when whoever finds it has obtained his or her true desires. Further, the talisman is not the sole medium whereby magical power materializes. In Katherine's adventure, Merlin also has access to power and is forced to deal with some of the unintended and ill-conceived effects of the talisman. Merlin's power is stronger than the talisman's. The wizard sets up new rules for the talisman's operation in order to contain the amount of mischief it can perpetrate in the future.

In *Half Magic*, magic is powerful, sometimes worrisome, and even destructive; however, unlike Nesbit, Eager really does not want his readers to contemplate the possibility of any serious or evil misapplication of power. He is content to indulge whimsically any child's "what if" imagining. Further, restricting himself to the benign applications of magical power and assuming that his readers want good to be done, he feels no compunction about arranging matters in the story so that power only temporarily disrupts the lives of ordinary people for the sake of helping them attain their heart's desire. Like Nesbit's stories, Eager's narrative is family-oriented, grounded in the presumption that a warm, supportive family life is really what most people ardently desire. Because Eager is an apt learner, *Half Magic* is a successful fantasy. It is internally consistent, and, despite its debt to Nesbit's fiction, it is not slavishly imitative, since its American setting, along with the other differences, gives Eager's story freshness and variety. Although inciting awe is not an important element in *Half Magic,* the American setting, which suggests familiarity and coziness, is quite effective in providing both a realistic counterpoint to the fantasy and an opportunity for reassuring identification. The story "works" because of its author's clever variations on several of Nesbit's techniques, its internal consistency, its humor, and its likable protagonists. In *Half Magic,* as in all his other narratives, Edward Eager had no intention of creating "serious" or "great" literature, just entertaining fantasy, and he was successful.

Although Jane Langton also favors Nesbit, her debt to the British author, unlike Eager's, is not obvious. Still, the influence of Nesbit can be readily distinguished in Langton's series concerning the Hall family, *The Diamond in the Window, The Swing in the Summerhouse, The Astonishing Stereoscope,* and *The Fledgling.* Like Nesbit's characters, Langton's Eleanor, Edward, and Georgie are able to embark upon adventures because the adults in charge, Uncle Freddy and Aunt Lily, although loving and caring, are conveniently absorbed in their own concerns and careers. They are inclined philosophically to grant the children maximum freedom to grow up and try their wings, and keep out of the way— but not entirely. For unlike Nesbit's adult characters, Uncle Freddy and Aunt Lily find themselves embroiled in several of the children's escapades, in particular, the humorous ones. Another feature borrowed from Nesbit is the rationalized magical medium that enables the Hall children to move back and forth between a fantasy world and Concord, the setting of the novels. Careful to attribute magic to several objects (a diamond, a stereoscope, a swing, and a goose), Langton also explains its source. In the first three books, the children receive the magical objects from Prince Krishna, a master magician and friend of Aunt Lily, who is very careful to spell out to the children the conditions under which the magic operates. As expected, the children have to learn, often humorously, to cope with these conditions. In *The Fledgling* the Goose Prince, touched by Georgie's yearning to fly, offers her the gift of flying, but she can use it only with the proviso that she admit graciously the necessity of growing up and that she cease fighting.

Nesbit's influence is also perceived in the respect the American writer shows for the intelligence and curiosity of her readers—respect perhaps most aptly illustrated by Langton's habit of sprinkling throughout her narratives references to the history of Concord, especially the lives and ideas of two well-known residents, Emerson and Thoreau. As a matter of fact, Langton incorporates into her plots these references even at the risk of alienating some of her young readers. By embodying within her characters two very different attitudes toward history—one, which sees it as invigorating and inspiring, and the other, as dead and useful only to lure tourist dollars—Langton effectively dramatizes and investigates the ways in which the different attitudes affect people. The resulting contrast accounts for much of the humor of the novels as well as their seriousness. Accordingly, Uncle Freddy's sincerity and habit of wondering how Emerson and Thoreau would have acted or what they might have thought of his handling of a situation may be occasionally embarrassing and disconcerting. Still, Langton is at pains to show through the transparent goodness of the Halls that Emersonian idealism can still inspire and motivate. Further, she seems to be insisting that what occurs in the Hall home and in Uncle Freddy's Concord College of Transcendentalist Knowledge, even when occasionally silly, constitutes a far more authentic response to Concord's legacy than the crass chamber-of-commerce attitude of Mr. Preek and Miss Prawn, rivals of Uncle Freddy and Aunt Lily, who dismiss Uncle Freddy's idealism as impractical and look upon their town's history merely as attractions for tourist dollars. Clearly, much more than Eager, Langton has picked up on that element in Nesbitian fantasy that underscores topics, or addresses moral concerns. By doing so, she risks offending some of her potential audience, yet to any reader who enjoys intellectual challenge, Langton's novels are stimulating.

Journey Fantasy

Introduction

Mixed fantasy in which the narrative involves a type of journey remains popular with both readers and writers. Such stories include the old and familiar—*Alice in Wonderland, The Wind in the Willows, Peter Pan, The Lion, the Witch and the Wardrobe, The Mouse and His Child, Fog Magic, The Phantom Tollbooth, Journey Outside, Under Plum Lake, Alpha Centauri*—as well as the more recent works, such as *Wrinkle in Time, Something Upstairs, Time Cat, Reluctant God, Jeremy Visick, Dry Sea,* and *Voices after Midnight.* Why journey fantasy should prove attractive and rewarding to writers is easy to understand. For one thing, a journey can occur only when there is an individual or individuals traveling from one place to another; thus, basic plotting and motivation are provided. Whether there have been more journey fantasies with multiple protagonists than those with individual ones or whether readers prefer one kind over the other would seem at first glance unimportant questions. Ravenna Helson, however, argues that during the Edwardian Age, British fantasists came to prefer multiple protagonists over single ones. Rather than attributing the change to coincidence or a move toward more complicated plot structures with multiple protagonists as pioneered by Nesbit, Helson contends that the preference she finds reflects a fundamental change in attitude; that is, the Edwardians, suffering a loss of confidence in the validity of "going it alone," began to experience, even in their literature for children, a growing dependence on the group ("Through the Pages," 107). Regardless of the merit of Helson's argument, recent fantasy shows no preference for either single or multiple protagonists. Moreover, it is not always clear whether a story has just one major protagonist-traveler. In *The Wonderful Wizard of Oz,* Dorothy sets off alone for the Emerald City because she wants to find a way to return to Kansas. In the course of her journey she befriends several individuals—a cowardly lion, a scarecrow, and a tin man—who decide they too need to go to Emerald City. Is Dorothy the only major character? Or are there now four major characters? Given the keen interest of children in pets, what about Toto, Dorothy's dog?

Because journeys usually occur for a reason, the writer is obliged to explain why a particular journey takes place; thus, motives and purposes have to be clarified. These can be quite ordinary: curious Alice wants to learn why a white rabbit, muttering "I'm late, I'm late," disappears down a hole; Greta in *Fog Magic* likes going for long walks on foggy days; Tom of *Tom's Midnight Garden* comes downstairs and checks to see if indeed the clock chimed thirteen; Robert and Jennifer, of *In the Circle of Time* by Margaret J. Anderson, dig to uncover any of three missing stones that may be nearby; and in Robert Siegel's *Alpha Centauri*, Becky, unable to wait till morning, sneaks out at night to take a ride on a horse. On the other hand, motives and purposes can be serious: Dilar in *Journey Outside* seeks to discover if what his grandfather said about a "better place" is true, Stuart Little must follow his dream; a mechanical toy in *The Mouse and His Child* is restored to working order by a tramp, wound up, and put down the road with the injunction "Be a tramp"; and the toy soldiers of *The Return of the Twelves* that once belonged to the Brontë children decide for safety's sake to return to their original home. Finally, a journey can be so serious and organized that it becomes a formal quest as, for instance, in C. S. Lewis's *The Voyage of the Dawn Treader,* when King Caspian, accompanied by three human children, sets sail to find out why seven Narnian lords failed to return from an important mission.

Defining a Journey Fantasy

A journey may or may not end where it began, but in moving from one point to another the character or characters must traverse a certain route, terrain, or distance. While doing so, the traveler may see something distinctive or awesome about the place through which he or she is passing; furthermore, on the way, the traveler is more than likely to undergo a number of experiences, some of which may constitute serious obstacles to the successful conclusion of the journey. All of these requirements give writers ample opportunity, depending upon their respective plots and preferences, to devise appropriate adventures and describe sites, landscape, scenery, and populace. In particular, the descriptions that are called for, besides being necessary to the plot, often provide the reader an interesting and welcome variety. For instance, after reading Norton Juster's *The Phantom Tollbooth,* who can forget Milo and Tock's visits to such bizarre places as "Expectations," "Dictionopolis," and "Foothills of

Confusion"? Readers also remember, long after reading George MacDonald's *At the Back of the North Wind*, Diamond's meeting of the Apostles
on one of his journeys with the North Wind. The Apostles, depicted in
stained glass, come alive as the moor lights brighten the church's windows. Also memorable are such events as found in C. S. Lewis's description in *The Lion, the Witch, and the Wardrobe* of the long-awaited coming
of spring, which had been denied Narnia for years by the wicked White
Queen; the absurd incidents in Russell Hoban's *The Mouse and His Child*,
in particular the shrews' and the wood mice's struggle and mutual slaughter; and, in Alan Garner's *Elidor*, the breakdown of the electrical system
in the Watson home while it is besieged by the spearmen from Elidor
wanting to seize the treasures hidden there.

The chief explanation, then, for the popularity of journey fantasy
may be the relative ease with which it supports and accommodates a
variety of incidents and inspires energetic storytelling. This ease, incidentally, is often attractive to beginning readers as well as anyone who
might experience difficulty in following a complicated plot structure.
The basic form of journey fantasy serves as an energizing force for both
the reader and writer; the obvious necessity of moving the protagonist
from one place to another furnishes not only a clear and forceful purpose that helps the author never to forget where the narrative is headed
but also provides a high potential for a variety of minor excursions.
These advantages of purpose and variety are even better appreciated if
one likens the basic structure of journey fantasy to a string upon which
beads of incident and adventure can be strung. By adopting this structural pattern, writers can carefully control the number of characters
and their functions, distinguishing those who aid or oppose the protagonist on his or her journey. The final advantage of this structural pattern is that it makes plausible and palatable descriptive passages ex-
tolling the "wonderfulness" of the actual journey, the terrain traversed,
or the locale visited. In this way, authors are not only assisted but encouraged to incorporate into their stories incidents and descriptions
that can incite awe or wonder.

The mode of transportation used by the protagonist, such as walking, riding a horse, or flying, is important in distinguishing between science fiction and fantasy. In order to make that distinction, a reader
must examine not only the journey itself but how the protagonist ar-

rived at the starting point of the journey. In both fantasy subtypes, modes of travel are virtually unlimited—with one important restriction: If the mode is scientifically rationalized, then the story is likely to be science fiction and not journey fantasy. Still, it is not always easy to distinguish between the two subtypes. In L'Engle's *A Wrinkle in Time*, the Murrys travel through space by means of a tesseract or wrinkle that appears to be a valid extrapolation from mathematical and physical principles; therefore, the novel is science fiction. On the other hand, because Meg is accompanied on her journeys by angels, whose existence is not validated by science, *A Wrinkle in Time* may be considered a fantasy. More about L'Engle's works of fantasy appears in chapter 4.

How the protagonist arrives at the point where the journey originates requires the author's careful attention. For Nesbit, this point is often a "weak spot" in the curtain separating the world of fantasy from the real world—the point where fantasy and reality impinge upon or bump into each other. Over the years, fantasists, accepting the challenge to be original, have vied with each other to come up with exciting, different means of moving from the one world to the other. For example, in *Tom's Midnight Garden*, a clock chiming thirteen and a long unopened door unexpectedly standing ajar allow Tom to walk into the special garden and the past. In *The Phantom Tollbooth*, Milo mysteriously receives a package, which he unwraps to reveal a tollbooth and an automobile which, when assembled, take the boy into a very distinctive fantasy land. In Lloyd Alexander's *The First Two Lives of Lukas-Kasha*, Lukas enters the kingdom of Abadan when, encouraged by the mountebank Battisto to look into a pail of water and see his fortune, he falls into the water and into Abadan. Jay Williams's *The Hero from Otherwhere* moves his characters, Rich and Jesse, into the fantasy land of Gwyliath through the magical door of the principal's office. In John Kier Cross's *The Other Side of Green Hills*, looking correctly at an optical illusion enables five children to learn that everything possesses "an In and an Out," and permits the mystical Owl and Pussycat to cross over and lead the children back to the "other side."

Two points remain. The places or lands traveled to in journey fantasy can be real (New York, New Amsterdam, Roman Britain, southern Ohio during the time of the Mound Builders) or imaginary (Narnia, Oz, Elidor, the Other Side) and the possibilities are endless.

Whether real or imaginary makes no difference to the fantasist, for the challenge in both instances remains the same: to re-create the place or land credibly and plausibly and, if describing an actual locale, to be as accurate as one can be, even if research is necessary; and to endow the place or land with details that will make it fresh and different so that the wonderful—that elusive but tangible quality—may be experienced. Lastly, the journey can involve traveling through and beyond time, hence time travel or time-slip fantasy. For some observers this subtype is quintessential children's fantasy, perhaps because some of the most distinctive children's fantasies of recent years have been time travel: Sauer's *Fog Magic*, the Green Knowe books, Pearce's *Tom's Midnight Garden*, Ormondroyd's *Time at the Top*, Farmer's *A Castle of Bone*, Uttley's *A Traveler in Time*, Lunn's *The Root Cellar*, Mayne's *A Game of Dark*, Bond's *A String in the Harp*, Park's *Playing Beatie Bow*, Cooney's *Both Sides of Time*, and L'Engle's *An Acceptable Time*.

One more of Nesbit's contributions to children's fantasy is her solution to a potentially irksome problem peculiar to time travel. How much real time elapses while the young protagonists enjoy their adventures into the past or future? Won't parents and other concerned adults worry about the lengthy disappearance of the children? Nesbit's solution was simple and has been subsequently adopted by most writers: no real time, or very little, elapses despite the length of the stay in the past or the future, whether a day or years. Nesbit's solution, it should be noted, is different from what usually occurs in fairy tales, where enchantment may force protagonists to reside for many years while their contemporaries age: Such was the fate of Rip Van Winkle, who awoke to find family, wife, and friends long dead.

Much of what has just been presented may be better understood if three journey fantasies, C. S. Lewis's *The Voyage of the Dawn Treader*, Mary Q. Steele's *Journey Outside*, and Julia Sauer's *Fog Magic*, are examined in some detail. The first is exemplary journey fantasy whose plot is relatively simple. Edmund and Lucy Pevensie, along with their cousin Eustace, are drawn into Narnia during young King Caspian's reign and become part of the fellowship he has gathered for two chief purposes: to explore the unknown Eastern Seas beyond the Longe Islands in Narnia, and to investigate what happened to seven Narnian lords, friends of Caspian's father, who had been sent out previously into the Eastern Seas. Reepicheep, the Talking Mouse and one of the fellowship, has an additional purpose for the journey, to ascertain whether Aslan's country is located at the boundaries of the Eastern Seas. As the three purposes are gradually intertwined, the journey of the *Dawn Treader* becomes one of discovery, search, and quest—one on which the travelers are likely to encounter wonder. Indeed, new lands are found or re-found but not before a series of adventures, some of them quite unexpected. For example, even before the journey actually begins, several of the fellowship are captured, enslaved, and need to be rescued. Interestingly, the three visitors in Narnia have no particular goal or purpose, nor are their functions predicted or preordained; however, they do assist their comrades in several key scenes. Further, what occurs is important for Edmund, Lucy, and Eustace's moral and spiritual growth.

The basic structure of *The Voyage of the Dawn Treader* is linear and chronological. As the ship sails east beyond the Longe Islands, the fellowship will discover exotic isles where they uncover evidence of the missing lords: Dragon Island, where one of the lords perished and Eustace is transformed into a dragon; Deathwater, where a pool of water turns anything touching it into gold and incites greed even in bystanders; the land of the absurd, lovable Dufflepuds, who regain visibility through the help of Lucy (who unexpectedly finds herself tempted by promises of great beauty and knowledge of the future); the "dark island," where dreams come true; and finally "the World's End," the outermost limits of the Eastern Seas, where three surviving lords are located and the company learns that one final option remains: an actual penetration into the "end of the world," the land of Aslan. Thus the linear structure readily accommodates the description and exposition necessary to flesh out the three purposes of the journey. Moreover, the sequence of incidents allows for character development. It gradually becomes clear that there are distinctly ethical and didactic dimensions to the story; with the exception of Edmund, each of the main characters is "tested" to determine whether he or she is worthy to continue on to the "end of the world."

Two incidents in particular illustrate the advantages of journey fantasy when the subtype is utilized by someone who appreciates, as Lewis does, its potential. In the episode that takes place on Dragon Island, for example, Lewis writes knowledgeably of dragon lore, both informing and contributing to the wonder of his narrative:

> Something *was* crawling. Worse still, something was coming out. . . . The thing that came out of the cave was something he had never even imagined—a long lead-coloured snout, dull red eyes, no feathers or fur, a long lithe body that trailed on the ground, legs whose elbows went up higher than its back like a spider's, cruel claws, bat's wings that made a rasping noise on the stones, yards of tail. And the two lines of smoke were coming from its two nostrils. (chapter VI)

A scene shocking to some readers, it is plausible inasmuch as the boy, Eustace, who already had been characterized as having the disposition of a dragon, magically is transformed into one and behaves accordingly when he eats a dead dragon. Further, the scene describing Eustace's return to human form provides graphic detailing of what the tearing off of dragon skin must feel like.

> The very first tear he made was so deep that I thought it had gone right into my heart. And when he began pulling the skin off, it hurt worse than anything I've ever felt. The only thing that made me able to bear it was just the pleasure of feeling the stuff peel off. You know—if you've ever picked the scab of a sore place. It hurts like billy—oh but it *is* such fun to see it coming away. (chapter VII)

This scene also provides necessary explication in which Lewis introduces Aslan, the giant lion, into the narrative, thereby underscoring its ethical-didactic dimension.

Another well-crafted scene concerns the fellowship's adventures with the Dufflepuds. Combined effortlessly and entertainingly are suspense, humor, significant characterization, and seriousness. Lewis establishes an aura of suspense with the mysterious disembodied voices that threaten harm unless Lucy helps them. He introduces humor both in the behavior of the vain Dufflepuds, who constantly interrupt their leader and change their minds, and in their unique bodily form, consisting of one large foot that allows them to hop easily on land and to float in the water like a canoe. He develops significant characterization through the unexpected temptation that Lucy faces, as she almost succumbs to the promise of beauty, gossip about her friends, and knowledge of the future but is saved by Aslan's intervention. Finally, he maintains the narrative's seriousness as it reveals the startling information about the wondrous island and its ruler, Coriakin, the magician.

Three relevant observations of *The Dawn Treader* remain. First, just when the fellowship arrives at the island where the three surviving lords are found and one expects the story to end, the reader is surprised with a second journey and the subsequent formation of another fellowship. This doubling is in some respects more interesting and provocative than the recounting of the first, longer journey. Second, because Lewis places the goal of the *Dawn Treader* in the east, the mystical land of origins, the end of the journey becomes paradoxically a new beginning for the chief characters. Reminded that as king his duty is foremost to his subjects, Caspian grudgingly agrees not to attempt a journey to the "end of the world." He returns home but not empty-handed since, it is hinted Ramandu's daughter will be his Queen. Reepicheep finds his "heart's desire" and is last seen entering into Aslan's land, while Lucy and Edmund, told that their adventures in Narnia are all over and having learned to recognize Aslan, are now prepared to know him in their own time and country. Only Eustace's destiny is left open-ended. Last, in speaking of the "end of the world" as a goal of Reepicheep and in describing the journey there as to actual places, Lewis engages in mythopoesis, utilizing a combination of traditional material and his own. Hence, the chapters with their evocation of the familiar, traditional, and mythic, along with Lewis's own original material, illustrate the fantasist's use of the "pot of story" and, as such, demonstrates graphically how journey fantasy can create fresh and imaginative storytelling.

Very different in its use of the journey format is Mary Q. Steele's *Journey Outside*, a novel that has been unfortunately neglected despite being honored as a Newbery Medal book. Dilar, a member of the Raft People who, beneath the mountains, ride a river flowing in a circle that takes approximately a year to complete, decides to abandon his people and seek the supposed "better place" they claim as the point of their constant voyaging. Before the boy comes to the end of his search, he enjoys a series of adventures among distinctively different peoples and locales: Dorna, Norna, and the other shepherds and pumpkin gatherers who, although living simply and well, are incapable of working and planning for winter and the scarcity of easily available food; Wingo, who lives high in the mountains and out of pity and concern for the small animals feeds them but closes his eyes to the fact that his feeding brings about their slaughter by larger animals; the Not People, who fatalistically subsist in a desert environment and consider themselves part of that environment; and Vigan, a goat herder who is at last able to give Dilar some answers to the questions he asks about the nature of his people and the purpose of life.

One impressive strength of Steele's story is its success in showing how a boy who knows only the darkness and dampness of caves barely lit by torches, without fresh air, sunlight, and wind, can find the color and sensations of everyday living outdoors both disorienting and exhilarating as he struggles to make sense of what he sees after coming above ground. For instance, the description of a bird flying toward Dilar further illustrates this.

> Something was coming toward him in the air, a little fish gliding through the air, helping itself along with great fins that stuck out from its sides and then folded tight against them. A wonder, a wonder! The fish stopped suddenly in the top of one of the little trees, put out little legs to hold itself up, threw back its head, and opening its mouth made such sounds as Dilar had never heard before. (chapter 3)

Steele uses the technique of displacement convincingly to assist readers in their ability to see the ordinary world around them as wonderful. Augmenting the wonder Dilar feels in the face of the ordinary and everyday is the genuine strangeness of the people and lands he encounters on his journey, such as the bizarre desert place inhabited by the Not People, "terribly thin, brown, leathery, pale-eyed, tangle-haired" (chapter 11). There is even a touch of humor in the bewildered Dilar's suspicion that the new world he has emerged into is a "country of fantasy" (chapter 3). Further, when the boy is told that his raft people have become legendary to the people above ground, he begins to suspect that his people may be cursed.

Another impressive strength of *Journey Outside* is its insight into some key aspects of growing up or coming of age. It soon becomes apparent that Dilar's quest involves not only helping his grandfather and the other Raft People learn what and where the "better place" is but also accomplishing something that Dilar senses is very important to himself. He is unable to articulate this sense until the very end, and even then what is said may not be eloquent, but it is valid. Dilar's moment of insight occurs only when Vigan, through a question-and-answer technique, draws out of the boy both understanding and acceptance of his real motives for the journey in light of what subsequently transpires. The climax occurs after Vigan sends Dilar to snatch an eagle's egg from its nest, a task the boy is driven to accomplish, at great personal risk, because he believes obtaining the egg will finally assure his receiving answers to his questions.

> "Ah, he is the wise man," thought Dilar, "I have been chosen then, and the egg will tell me what the magic is. It is like the stories. I have been given a task and I have done it, in spite of danger and hardship, and now I will have passed the test and I will know the answers." (chapter 14)

Shocked when Vigan proceeds to eat the hard-earned egg, the boy protests that he has been used. Vigan, however, points out that his trick enabled the boy to "do a difficult and dangerous thing" that ought to give him pleasure and in any case is the "reason for being young and strong." Almost against his will, Dilar is forced to agree and gradually does feel "proud and sure of himself."

After Vigan presents a probable explanation for the Raft People's way of life, Dilar reaffirms his initial goal. "I want to bring my people out into the world again! . . . I want to show them how stupid they have been." Surmising that apparently Dilar has learned nothing from his various experiences, especially any important insight into human nature, the old man points out: "All men are wise about one thing or another—and all men are stupid about an equal number of things." When Dilar insists that he indeed wants to help his grandfather come to a "better place" and enjoy the beauty of the aboveground, Vigan objects. For him, that reason is not good enough. Pushed about as far as he can tolerate, the boy suddenly recalls what Vigan had earlier stated—performing difficult and dangerous deeds is the reason for being young and strong—and blurts out his final reason for returning: "Because." Finally pleased, Vigan agrees that is reason enough. When the boy departs, the old man calls him back, not to give him some magical object, as the boy hopes, but to confide that, if he had a grandson, he would want him to be like Dilar. Thus, the affection and support from an old man to a young boy are key in assisting Dilar to grasp the meaning of what has happened to him on his quest. Further, that there exists a web of understanding and support between generations is the final insight of the novel: To be young is to do and love; to be old is to support and love.

Journey Outside is a fine example of how journey fantasy, which is in many respects a traditional story format, can be adapted for the contemporary purpose of bringing home to young readers the unique advantages of their physical strength which, among other things, enables them to have adventures. Furthermore, *Journey Outside* assures young readers that, even if growing up must involve ethical and moral maturation, as well as doing something good that adults insist on or approve of, it is still right for youth to feel good about itself for being young, strong, and open to adventure. Therefore, why go adventuring? Why climb mountains? Why go backpacking cross-country? Because! *Journey Outside*, then, furnishes a helpful, perhaps necessary, corrective to adults, reminding them not to insist that the didactic strain in children's fantasy reinforce just those aspects of growing up that adults deem important or proper.

Julia Sauer's *Fog Magic*, another contemporary fantasy, is journey fantasy on two counts. First, journeys from her home in Little Valley, a village in Nova Scotia, through the fog, down the Post Road, and to a neighboring village are important elements in the story of eleven-year-old Greta Addington, the protagonist. More importantly, the young girl's trips are also time travel inasmuch as Greta can only enter Blue Cove as it existed in the past, for in the present it is deserted and in ruins. Sauer incorporates fog, so common on the Nova Scotia coast, prominently into her story as setting and occasion for magic. The importance of fog is introduced very early as Sauer informs readers that Greta from infancy felt attracted to it and wanted to be out in it as often as she could. An old neighbor even calls her "fog-struck," a characteristic almost frightening to Greta's mother. *Fog Magic*, like *Journey*

Outside, involves coming of age or "safe passage," as Mrs. Morrill, one of the Blue Cove inhabitants, refers to the passage from childhood to adulthood. Interestingly, in her presentation of feminine coming of age, Sauer avoids explicit psychologizing, preferring indirection and implication; her forte as a writer is her delicacy and sensitivity.

Of special interest is the care with which Sauer sets out the rules by which Greta can time travel. For one thing, she can proceed down the road to Little Cove only when she can trace in the fog the dark outline of a house that functions as a "sort of magic beacon" (chapter 2). In its absence she must turn back, for the magic beacon "was always to be trusted. Disobey its message and there was a long walk, but nothing more" (chapter 2). Another rule is that, although real time can pass swiftly between Greta's excursions into the past, sometimes whole weeks, when finally she manages to return to the Morrills in Blue Cove, usually it is just the next day. Moreover, when the fog definitely begins to lift, Greta must leave. Generally speaking, she cannot take anything out of the past into her time, and she must be careful not to injure herself while in the past because—and no explanation is given—she cannot be helped. She must not inform the Morrills of what happens to either individuals or the village as a whole. Once or twice Greta does divulge information, but the villagers ignore her or are upset. The final rule Sauer designates is that on her twelfth birthday Greta loses the ability to time travel. To compensate partially for that loss, she discovers that her father as a boy had also been able to time travel; hence, father and daughter can share memories and take pleasure in having been able to visit Blue Cove.

Sauer has her characters abide by the rules. Yet, almost as if suspecting that the rules and her characters' strict compliance with them makes for fantasy perhaps too rationalized and mechanical, she incorporates two elements that enhance wonder. The fog is one element, since it is both a romantic setting against which so much of the book's action takes place and an agency for the working of magic: "Fog had always seemed . . . like the magic spell in the old fairy tales—a spell that caught you up and kept you as safe, once you were inside it, as you would have been within a soap bubble" (chapter 1).

The second element is the poignancy and sadness evident in the realization that the people of Blue Cove are somehow trapped between the past and the future. Still alive in the past, they cannot avoid accepting that periodically they are visited by individuals from the future and must wait patiently for a new generation of Addingtons to commence visiting them. At the same time, the inhabitants of Blue Cove do not want to know what the future has in store for them; they are people who somehow "have to learn to be content and at peace, shut in by their horizon" (chapter 6).

Understanding Other Cultures and Time Periods through Fantasy

Time-slip fantasy offers readers the opportunity to discover, learn, and develop understandings about other cultures and time periods. Authors such as Kevin Major, Caroline Cooney, Lloyd Alexander, Pamela Service, and Jane Yolen have successfully created time-slip fantasies that are richly embedded with the detail and drama of the time.

Kevin Major creates a poignant story about the Beothuk Indian culture of Newfoundland in *Blood Red Ochre*. Filled with mystery and suspense, this young adult novel explores the last days of a culture and its people's attempt to save it. David, a fifteen-year-old male, meets Nancy in a high school class. He is fascinated by her and they quickly begin a friendship that culminates in a canoe trip back in time to Red Ochre Island—a burial ground of the Beothuk Indians. Throughout the story, Major moves the reader between the present and the past by alternating chapters from David (present day) to Dauoodaset (past). The reader is able to view the personal and cultural conflicts that each young man must face, while Nancy—who exists in both the present and the past—acts as a conduit between time periods and cultures.

Enchanted by a mansion on the verge of being torn down and disillusioned by her controlling boyfriend, ninth-grade Annie Lockwood muses about life in an earlier time. "I am a romantic in the wrong century, she thought. I live in the 1990s. I should be in the 1890s. I bet I could have found true love a hundred years ago" (7). So begins Caroline Cooney's novel *Both Sides of Time*.

Annie Lockwood is transported back through time by a force seemingly outside of her control. "It was as strong as gravity. It had a grip, and seized her ankles . . . It was beneath her—the power was from below—taking her down. Not through the floor, but through— through what?" (13). Upon arriving in her new time, Annie appears first as a ghost and then later gains solid form. She describes her experience, recognizing that she is not alone in experiencing time slips. "I could feel the time rushing past my face. There were other people in there with me. Half people. I'm not the only one changing centuries, thought Annie. Other bodies and souls flew past me. Or with me. Or through me" (43).

Drawn by the romance of the time and the very attractive current resident of the mansion, eighteen-year-old Hiram Stratton Jr., Annie decides right then and there to stay. She soon becomes a part of the life of the aristocratic nineteenth century and the events surrounding a mysterious murder. With sadness but a sense of obligation, Annie decides to return to the twentieth century, but when her father dismisses her mother's opinion it hits her in a rush. "It was the brush that did it for Annie. That physical sweep of the arm, getting rid of the annoying female opinion. She could see a whole long century of men brushing their wives aside" (138). Her father grounds her for disappearing and scaring them all. Sean, her boyfriend, forgives her, and she is indignant and convinced that she must return in time to Strat. Back in the past, Annie slowly realizes that she must again return to the present. Because she has been given some powers over time, she recognizes that with those powers comes the obligation to serve as a "century changer" (208) and that hers is a feminist mission. "Annie had tasted both sides of time, and each in its way was so cruel to women. But she must not be one of the women who caused cruelty; she must be one who eased it" (206). The somewhat weak conclusion ends mid-journey back to the present and leaves the reader to imagine where Annie ends up and what happens when she gets there.

In Lloyd Alexander's *Time Cat*, subtitled "The Remarkable Journeys of Jason and Gareth," a black cat named Gareth has the ability to speak and to travel through time. Gareth announces to his young friend Jason (who has had a particularly bad day) that he doesn't have nine successive lives, but rather, "I can visit nine different lives. Anywhere, any time, any country, any century" (3).

With the wink of an eye, boy and cat are transported to Egypt, 2700 B.C., for their first of nine "lives." Each life brings new adventure, danger, and learning. The reader learns along with the main character, Jason, about people and their civilizations from how they treat young strangers and, in particular, cats. We are encouraged to observe and to think carefully, regardless of how well we think we might know something already. "But just because you've seen something, it doesn't mean you stop looking. There's always something you didn't see before," Gareth tells Jason (100).

From the best, Egypt, where cats were considered sacred, to the worst, Germany, where cats were believed to be inhabited by devils and people were convicted of witchcraft if caught with a cat, we observe nine different civilizations and learn along with Jason. Gareth's final "life" takes them to America in 1775, where a traveling peddler sells and distributes kittens throughout the countryside. Gareth tells Jason just before returning home, "There's a certain moment that comes— even for a kitten—when you have to start thinking about growing up. That's a very special occasion. It begins by learning new things" (203). He continues, "The journey isn't over. If you want to know the truth, it's really just starting. You'll make your own voyages even farther" (204).

Gareth tells Jason that when they return they will no longer be able to speak to one another but that they will be able to communicate by watching and observing closely. The novel ends with Jason back in his own bed, disappointedly believing that the travels had been merely a dream until he discovers, deep in his pocket, an ankh from his journey. Armed with the confidence to think for himself, he goes downstairs for supper.

In another time-slip fantasy, author Pamela Service chooses to move her character forward in time in *The Reluctant God*, in which teenagers from two cultures four thousand years apart are drawn together to unravel the mystery surrounding the expectations of ancient gods. Lorna Padgett is the twentieth-century teenage daughter of an archeologist who stumbles upon the four-thousand-year-old Egyptian tomb of a pharaoh's son. Without imagining the consequences, the archeology group moves the belongings of the tomb—including the seemingly solid stone sarcophagus—to the city of Cairo. Housed in an archeological institute where Lorna and her father have living quarters, the sarcophagus suddenly breaks open following a powerful clap of thunder during a storm. Lorna is surprised to find a figure, which she assumes to be a wax figure covering a mummy, of a young man about her own age.

Reading the hieroglyphics inscribed on the inside of cover, she is struck by the familiarity of the name and the apparent royal lineage of the boy. Racing downstairs to the library, she finds the information about the royal family and returns to the room only to find the figure gone and the window of the room open. After a night of fear and confusion as to the fate of the "mummy," Lorna is further stunned when he reappears at her front door the next day—fully alive and seeking her help. Thus begins the adventures of Lorna and Ameni—the pharaoh's son who was sealed in the tomb by the high priests of his time and released into the twentieth century to guard and secure eternity for his people.

Service does an excellent job of combining historical information with mystery and intrigue through the venue of a time-slip fantasy. Although her characters do not travel back and forth across time, she does bring the past forward through Ameni's call upon his ancient gods for help. Readers are allowed a view of ancient Egypt through the eyes of Ameni, and the believability of the experiences lend credibility to the adventure.

A final time-slip fantasy that connects the past and present through historical and cultural experiences is Jane Yolen's *The Devil's Arithmetic*. This powerful story uses the means of time slip to propel the protagonist, Hannah, back into the days of World War II and the Holocaust. The story begins with Hannah and her parents on route to visit her grandparents and other relatives for the feast of Passover. Although Hannah participates with her family in the Seder, she is less than enthusiastic about the rituals and virtually unaware of the importance of the "remembering." Her lack of sincerity is evident, yet her parents and relatives insist on her participation. Hannah feels that her grandfather is half crazy, throwing fits and shaking his fists at the TV screen full Nazi war camps. Hannah is embarrassed by her grandfather's actions and does not understand why he continues to rant about things of the past. She is comforted by her Aunt Eva, yet does not understand why her aunt chose to remain unmarried and live with her brother and his wife. Further, she feels like a fraud when asked to open the door to Elijah the prophet—an act in which she does not believe. Out of obligation, however, she does as her grandfather asks and is thrust back in time to the horrors of the Holocaust. Yolen creates strong characters in Hannah, known in the past as Chaya; Rivka, later known as Aunt Eva;

and Wolfe, later known as Hannah's Grandfather Will—all of whom play significant roles in the reader's ability to learn and better understand the terrible events of that time period. By using time-slip fantasy as a way to move Hannah from present day to the past, we can better experience the Holocaust tragedy in ways not available through history books. The people and events are made real to the reader, and the tie to Hannah's present life and relatives is believable, though mysterious and ominous. As Yolen states in her brief essay at the end of the book:

> Fiction cannot recite the numbing numbers, but it can be that witness, that memory. A storyteller can attempt to tell the human tale, can make a galaxy out of the chaos, can point to the fact that some people survived even as most people died. And can remind us that the swallows still sing around the smokestacks.

Time-slip fantasy allows us, as readers, to visit other times, other cultures, and other human experiences with a level of sensitivity that is absent from history books. Although fantasy and fiction have often been dismissed as frivolous by those unfamiliar with it, few who have read time-slip fantasies such as those discussed could dismiss the cultural and human values implicit within them.

Transformation Fantasy

Our daily lives are bombarded with advertisements that push us to change or transform who we are, where we live, what we do, and how we do it. Whether we fantasize about winning the lottery or daydream about how a new product will improve our sex appeal, it is human nature to wish to be something we are not. These fantasies begin in childhood with imaginary friends and creative role playing through games of make-believe. These same creative desires can be fed through transformation fantasy that provides opportunities for young people to enter worlds where animals think, talk, and behave in human terms and where size and form are relative.

Transformation fantasy may be divided into four types: from an inanimate into an animate; from animate to real; change in size; and human beings who change shape or form. In the first the inanimate state of the protagonist is altered into an animate one: A subsequent change may involve the protagonist's acquiring locomotion. For instance, in Carlo Collodi's *Pinocchio*, Geppetto carves a block of wood into a marionette; then because of the woodcarver's great desire for a son and the Blue-Haired Fairy's intervention, the marionette attains consciousness and the ability to walk about without any controlling strings. Not every fantasy of this subtype follows the two-step sequence, although most do; moreover, there can be many variations in depicting the sequence. The gaining of consciousness, for example, may have occurred before the story actually begins, as in *Miss Hickory*, where the doll already can think and move when the action begins to unfold. Oddly, the doll cannot completely turn her head, because it was originally attached to an apple wood twig and it retains some of that rigidity. Also, having literally lost her head to a squirrel, Miss Hickory manages somehow to cling to an old Macintosh apple tree, where she undergoes a second change, becoming a scion grafted to the tree. The author, Carolyn Bailey, does not furnish the why and wherefore of the doll's transformation, content to attribute the change to magic. In Rachel Field's *Hitty: Her First Hundred Years*, on the other hand, Hitty, a six-and-a-half inch doll fashioned from a lucky piece of mountain ash wood, only gains consciousness after the Old Peddler paints a face on the wooden doll he has been carving as a gift for a young girl, Phoebe Primble. The objects that come alive in the first type of transformation fantasy are often common, everyday objects such as nuts, fans, matches, chess pieces, playing cards, chairs, thimbles, blocks, and (understandably, given the prime audience) favorite dolls and toys of all kinds. Like Andersen before him, L. Frank Baum was especially imaginative in utilizing for his stories common household objects, as in the various items found in the *Who's Who in Oz*. Less often the objects attaining consciousness and locomotion are relatively uncommon or inconveniently sized, such as the marble statues in Nesbit's *The Enchanted Castle*, stone gargoyle animals in Georgess McHargue's *Stoneflight*, story illustrations in Humphrey Carpenter's *The Captain Hook Affair*, paper cutouts in Laurence Yep's *Dragon of the Lost Sea*, and television cartoon characters in Pierre Berton's *The Secret World of Og*.

In the second type of transformation fantasy, the change the protagonist undergoes involves a natural or logical extension of type one. The protagonist, having become animate and able to move around, continues to change, ultimately becoming real. Probably the most famous instance of this kind of alteration is again Pinocchio, who is magically transformed into the son for whom Geppetto fervently wished. The Blue-Haired Fairy's magic "merely" validates what Pinocchio has already exhibited: He is a "real" son willing to sacrifice his life for his father's, thereby demonstrating not only his freedom from any kind of controlling strings that literally and figuratively compel behavior and restrict independence, but also his freely bestowed love for Geppetto. Although not as universally known as Pinocchio, Margery Williams's *The Velveteen Rabbit* may be more useful than Collodi's classic in exemplifying the second type of transformation fantasy and clarifying its potentially great appeal to young readers.

The subtitle of Williams's work, "How Toys Become Real," indicates what the author intends. First, in her story about a small boy who, singling out a velveteen rabbit as his favorite toy and not wanting ever to be separated from it, eventually discards it in spite of having come to look upon it as "real," Williams is capitalizing on the intense affection most children have for favorite toys, becoming often emotionally dependent upon them and pretending that they are real. Second, Williams suggests an answer to the question many children ask: What really happens to a favorite toy after I stop playing with it or lose it or break it? Williams's answer is an engaging and ultimately satisfying mythopoesis. Early in the narrative, the Ski Horse explains to the newcomer in the nursery that toys become "real" to the children who love and need them because love, which is freely bestowed by children, gives the toys worth, while the needs they satisfy render them important to themselves and to children. The Ski Horse, however, warns the Rabbit that becoming real takes time, can hurt, and may involve losing some of the very features that made the toy initially lovable. Although soon becoming real in the boy's eyes, the Rabbit is surprised and confused to learn that it is not real like the rabbits outside that it once met. Subsequently, having grown old and shabby and having been discarded on a rubbish heap, the Rabbit turns despondent, questioning the point of becoming "real." In its despondency, it magically sheds a single real tear which, falling to the soil, engenders a flower that upon opening is mysteriously transformed into a fairy. Confronting the Rabbit, the fairy discloses that she is the "nursery magic Fairy" who cares for "all the playthings that the children have loved." She goes on to add that when "they are old and worn out and the children don't need them any more, then I come and take them away with me and turn them into Real." "Real," she points out, means that the Rabbit is not only real to the boy but also real to everyone. Williams's touching mythopoesis exemplifies and justifies the second type of transformation fantasy, especially its potential for satisfying a common yearning of childhood.

In the third type of transformation fantasy, characters or objects unexpectedly grow larger than normal or shrink, often becoming miniaturized. Lewis Carroll's *Alice in Wonderland* is the classic example as Alice alternately grows gigantic or shrinks into almost nothing because of food she eats or liquid she drinks. Other examples can be found in more recent stories. Mrs. Pepperpot, the little old woman in *Mrs. Pepperpot to the Rescue* by Alf Proysen, for no good reason shrinks to the size of a pepperpot and just as disconcertingly returns to her normal size. Oskar in Lucy Boston's *The River at Green Knowe* decides to make a nest similar to a harvest mouse's; working at it from the inside, he, along with the nest, inexplicably shrinks until he is just two inches tall, evidence of the river's powerful magic. In a final example found in Jane Curry's *The Mysterious Shrinking House*, we meet the protagonist Wilhelm Kurtz. Rejected many years before by the inhabitants of Dopple and in particular by Miss Mary Buckle, whose hand in marriage he had sought, Wilhelm Kurtz decides out of chagrin and petulance to turn his uncle's shrinking machine, originally intended to eradicate warts and other undesirable growths, on Dopple. He shrinks all its buildings and the people within to doll size. Kurtz also miniaturizes Mindy and her newly acquired dollhouse, including them as part of his Lilliput U.S.A. The remainder of Jane Curry's charming story focuses on Mindy and her new friends extricating themselves from Kurtz's control and returning via magnification to their proper size.

The focus of the fourth type of transformation is almost exclusively on human beings whose shape or nature is altered in some important way and then restored to its original form. Falling back upon special survival skills he learned through his magical transformations into bird, fish, deer, and mole, Tinykin of Mark Lemon's *The Enchanted Doll and Tinykin's Transformations* is able to release the Princess Udigu from her enchantment and wins her hand in marriage. As part of the action of

The Wind on the Moon by Eric Linklater, Dinah and Dorinda, the naughty daughters of Major and Mrs. Palfrey, change into kangaroos who are captured and placed in a private zoo from which they manage to escape and become girls again. Harry Houdini Marco of Zilpha Keatley Snyder's *Black and Blue Magic* is able to sprout wings and fly around San Francisco whenever he rubs on his shoulders drops from a silver bottle of lotion given to him by the mysterious Mr. Mazzeeck, a family friend. And in Andre Norton's *Fur Magic*, Cory Alter accidentally desecrates an Indian holy cache and must be purified; in the process, he is transformed into Yellow Shell, an animal, and out of necessity learns how to survive by living off and in cooperation with the land and its spirits—a lesson he successfully transfers to his life as a human.

Incidentally, the popular fantasy, *Stuart Little*, is also an instance of the fourth subtype, except that the diminutive hero never completes the sequence of change. While in his mother's womb, Stuart is inexplicably transformed into a mouse, and all his life he harbors intensely human feeling but never regains human form. Another well-known story that may come to mind as transformation fantasy is Andersen's "The Ugly Duckling." The story, however, is not transformational fantasy of any kind, for the so-called duckling is really a swan that has been mistakenly identified, and the swan it "changes" into is its natural self. Such a misunderstanding would be of no importance except that some adults like to point to "The Ugly Duckling" as a strongly hopeful, supportive fantasy that lends itself to bibliotherapy. Yet, the tale is not of some terrible physical or psychological limitation. Rather, it is one that ostensibly advocates patience under adverse circumstances. Critics know that beneath the surface level of this story runs Andersen's petulance and impatience with the slowly accelerating tempo of public recognition and honor given his work.

In transformation fantasy, considered as a whole, the change magically effected often seems to have no point other than supplying the germ for a good tale and hopefully inciting wonder. For example, nearly all of the Oz transformations are arbitrary, regardless of their charm. In Pauline Clarke's *The Return of the Twelves*, for another example, the twelve toy soldiers, which had been a gift to Brandon Brontë, quicken into life magically through the combined wishes, imagination, and efforts of Brandon and his sisters, Charlotte, Anne, and Emily, who, deciding to become Genii, construct an elaborate history and context whereby the lives of the toy soldiers are sustained and guided. In the elaborate arrangement set up between the Genii and the toy soldiers, Clarke intended merely to rationalize the latter's transformation; she makes no other point nor does she underscore any theme. In *Stuart Little* there seems to be no particular reason, other than its delightful absurdity, for the Littles' son to have been transformed into a mouse. On the other hand, in *Pinocchio* and *The Velveteen Rabbit*, as has been noted, the radical alteration parallels and validates the important psychological and emotional changes that are explicitly discussed in the story as not only possible but desirable. Plot and theme, then, can be wedded—sometimes blatantly, other times implicitly.

Roald Dahl almost brutally expresses in his *The Magic Finger* his contempt for hunting. The protagonist, a nameless eight-year-old girl, is capable, when incensed, of pointing her finger at whoever angers her and transforming that individual into something else. Accordingly, she changes a rude, and insensitive teacher, Mrs. Winter, into a rat, and because the girl cannot abide hunters, she transforms the Greggs, a family fond of hunting, into ducks and arranges for them, in turn, to be hunted. At the end of the story, the Coopers, another family that has angered the girl, is in imminent danger of being altered into something undesirable. The various transformations are designed to make Dahl's point that hunting is cruel. However, and more significantly, the didactic intent of *The Magic Finger* does not compensate for its conniving with a young reader's desire to strike back and hurt those who have offended him or her. Whatever Dahl may have intended, the strong anti-hunting message cannot disguise the girl's obvious glee in her power to change and hurt people.

In *The Mouse and His Child*, a less obviously didactic and more sophisticated narrative than *The Magic Finger*, Russell Hoban also takes pains to ensure that readers discern thematic implications in his story of the wind-up mouse and its child and their desire to be self-winding. Hoban makes a statement in his story of transformation by including the thematic features of beginning a journey, acquiring independence and family, problem-solving, and sustaining the family unit. He further supports this statement by establishing the Christmas season as the framing device in which the story opens and closes. Hence, various and sometimes contradictory themes can be distinguished. One would hardly claim that *The Mouse and His Child* is didactic celebration of self-reliance and family life, although Hoban manages to offset much of the impact of the violent and depressing incidents of the first half of the book (passages that rank among the most brutal and dispiriting ones in all of children's literature) with the very warm, emotionally satisfying, and gratifying depictions of family life and personal achievement in the second half. Instead of moralizing about being good, patient, and plucky if one wants a happy life, Hoban is content to incorporate into the story wit, insight, and compassion that may or may not be seized upon and internalized by individual readers.

Talking Animals

Stories about talking animals have been around for a long time, and various reasons for the longevity of these stories and their popularity have been proposed.

1. The interest many people take in animals, their wanting to be near them, and their affection for them;
2. A conviction that all creatures sharing a common habitat and possibly a common destiny should be as close to one another as possible;
3. A hunch that humanity can see itself adequately reflected in animal behavior;
4. A desire to communicate with animals because, it is felt, once in some long-ago golden and innocent era, all species on Earth were able to speak with or at least understand each other;
5. The suspicion that animals can communicate among themselves and choose for their own reasons not to speak to human beings; and
6. The belief that because homo sapiens is the superior species on Earth, it is only a matter of time before it achieves some kind of breakthrough in communicating with the lower species.

All these reasons, it should be noted, do not distinguish between young and old readers. Is there any explanation specific to children that may account for stories about animals in general and talking animals in particular becoming a staple of children's literature?

With the profound change in attitudes toward children commencing in the eighteenth century and climaxing in the next, along with the growing sentimentality in the treatment of animals that developed in the second half of the nineteenth century, animals, especially in their new role as pets, came to be perceived as apt providers of companionship for children. They also offered opportunities for the children to learn responsibility by taking care of them. Hence, stories about animals, in particular, dogs and horses, began to be written for children. Further, because they are clearly didactic as well as entertaining, beast fables have long been deemed especially appropriate for youngsters. Quite possibly children developed close relationships with small animals because they could identify and empathize with their comparable size, circumstances, and vulnerability. This relationship also many have prompted books about animals and children or about the possibility of their communicating with each other. For these reasons, then, animals, including talking ones, became part of the subject matter of books deemed suitable for children.

Realistic Portrayal of Animals
It is only fair to expect that the author (and illustrator, if the story contains pictures) should know something about the actual habits and character of the particular animal or animals he or she is writing about. Although fantasy can take extreme liberty with the actuality of animal life and behavior—horses, dogs, cats, pigs, mice, spiders, or whatever—the full impact of the story and its success as fantasy depend upon the accuracy of the information about animals undergirding the story. For instance, some of the humor and bite of *The Wind in the Willows* stems from the vain Toad's belief that the gaoler's daughter is romantically interested in him despite what the reader realizes is his squat, generally unpleasant physical appearance (at least as far as humans go). That Freddy, a pig and master sleuth, attempts to disguise his formidable porcine shape under a variety of costumes contributes to the zany appeal of *Freddy and the Baseball Team from Mars* and the other Freddy stories by Walter R. Brooks. The charm of *Charlotte's Web* derives in part both from the discrepancy between the connotations of some of the

names and the animals assigned them, such as a rapacious rat named Templeton, and from the appropriateness of other names given some of the characters—a pig and spider called Wilbur and Charlotte respectively. And the cumulative power of *The Animals of Farthing Wood* by Colin Dann is that, as they struggle to reach a new home in White Deer Park and develop a strong sense of community, each of the animals involved—fox, owl, adder, kestrel, toad, mole, weasel, and hare—behaves as everyone knows such animals would. Of course, with creatures of the imagination like a unicorn, a dragon, a phoenix, Nesbit's psammead, Lofting's pushmi-pullyu (the Dr. Dolittle stories), Alexander's gwythaint (the Prydain Chronicles), and Patricia Coombs's grompet (*Lisa and the Grompet*), there is no distinction to be made between misinformation and fantasy, but the writer establishes "common knowledge" about the creatures he or she invents.

Attributing Voice and Emotion to the Animal Kingdom

The assumption that animals cannot speak among themselves or to human beings is the foundation for all talking animal fantasy. However, for individuals who believe animals and humans can communicate somehow, perhaps even speak, talking animal fiction is not fantasy but realism—a very gray area. Is *Black Beauty* realism or mixed fantasy? Further, can an author, intending to write realistically about animals, insist upon entering their consciousness? Or must these authors, if they are to be successful, restrict themselves to remaining outside animal consciousness, as Jean Craighead George does in *Julie of the Wolves*? Sentimentality sometimes intrudes in realistic animal stories, causing some authors to assign to the animals feelings they may not be capable of or the authors have no sure way of determining. But in fantasy this problem does not exist, and fantasists can give their animal characters, as they have done now for some time, as broad a range of feelings and sentiments as human beings are capable of. Instead, the problems facing fantasists, as has been noted, are respecting the boundary between animals and humans, and developing plausible and consistent explanations for violating that boundary.

Content and Context of Animal Speech

If animals are depicted as talking, just what will they be talking about? If the animals are cast pretty much as human types (i.e., possessing enough human characteristics so that readers may identify with them), then the content of their conversations, in addition to such matters as food and attaining it, climate, or safety, must be of interest to human beings. This may all seem obvioius, yet authors of successful talking-animal fantasy do not overlook the point. The animals in Robert Lawson's *Rabbit Hill* worry that the new human family moving into a neighboring empty farmhouse may be hostile to them. Likewise, in Ben Lucien Burman's *Seven Stars for Catfish Bend*, the animals mostly discuss the threat of hunters and argue over ways of keeping out interlopers. Even in E. B. White's *Charlotte's Web*, one of whose rules is that Fern can only overhear the animals' conversation, not participate in it, White is careful to incorporate into the barnyard talk what Fern and the reader find most interesting—Wilbur, his continuing survival, and the ways Charlotte assists him to survive. What gives *Watership Down* much of its distinctiveness is Richard Adams's skill in creating a rabbit mythology that both fascinates any reader appreciative of mythopoesis and explains, plausibly in large part, what rabbits do and how they behave—at least, to be precise, to a human observer's eyes. Moreover, Adams has the rabbits spend a considerable amount of time talking about feeding (including defecating and despoiling their warren), finding new warrens, organizing and governing themselves, and setting up defensive arrangements—topics rabbits would discuss, if they could speak and if human behavior were natural to them.

Like *Watership Down*, Avi's series of the mid 1990s continues the use of animal mythology and its fascination for children. Young readers engage with the adventures of Poppy, Rye, and Periloo as these protagonists face the "human-like" challenges of their own world.

Categories of Animal Stories
In her fascinating and somewhat idiosyncratic study of humanized animals in literature, *Animal Land: The Creatures of Children's Fiction*, Margaret Blount has proposed a variety of ways to categorize the many stories in which animals are important characters. What has to be kept in mind when attempting to apply Blount's categories is that she cast her net as broadly as possible, including realistic adult fiction, so-called all-ages fantasy, and children's fantasy. Hence not all of her categories are useful here: Only those that illuminate children's mixed fantasy featuring talking animals will be commented on or adapted.

1. Animal Behavior as Allegory

Moral or didactic tales—traditional stories like beast fable and folk tale—often focus on animal behavior to point out how comparable behavior in human beings is mischievous or may lead to trouble, even destruction. Such tales, proliferating during the period from the seventeenth to the nineteenth centuries, are aptly modeled by stories such as Charles Kingsley's *The Water-Babies* and even *Pinocchio*. Their popularity has waned in recent years, but tales utilizing animal behavior as allegory of human behavior continue to appear. Examples in novel length are Beverley Nichols's *The Tree that Sat Down* and *The Stream that Stood Still* and the far more popular *The Sword in the Stone* by T. H. White, in which Wart, the future King Arthur, learns the kingly craft in part by becoming various animals and assimilating their skill, guile, and wisdom. Briefer examples are Randall Jarrell's *The Animal Family* and Arnold Lobel's *Fables*. Another once-popular subtype that featured human bodies literally or figuratively topped by animal heads might be ignored today except that Lewis Carroll, in the creation of his Wonderland, was influenced by this kind of animal story—an influence readily discernible in the semi-human faces of Carroll's animals that disguise, Blount suggests, "various aspects of human eccentricity, gaiety, sadness, tragedy and childish quirks" (78). Often children do not consider these animals amusing, while many adults find them comically familiar and self-reflective. Further, this type of animal story directly contributed to the origin of the comic or "funny paper" animal: Thus Mickey Mouse, Donald Duck, Bugs Bunny, Tom and Jerry, and similar animal characters can trace their ancestry to the early nineteenth-century fondness for employing animals comically to comment on human behavior, especially in stories aimed at children.

2. Mythical-Magical Beasts

Another type of talking animal fantasy features mythical-magical beasts, in particular, ones that can grant wishes, whose existence can be traced back to the bestiaries of ancient Egypt, Greece, and Asia Minor. Blount attributes the longevity of these beasts and their presence in fantasies today to their function as a kind of "face saving" for some people; although these people understand the world far more accurately and scientifically than did their ancestors, still they seem to need using expressions like "in a way," "perhaps," "supposing," whereby they can express their sense that there is a dimension to life not completely explained by rationally attained knowledge (96). Put another way, magic-granting animals allow both young and old readers to accommodate their longing for other, non-scientifically sanctioned dimensions in human life.

Mrs. Molesworth may have been the first writer to take a mythical-magical animal out of a fairy tale setting and place it in a realistic or contemporary setting: the cuckoo in *The Cuckoo Clock* and Dudu the Raven in *The Tapestry Room*. Unfortunately, being first does not always assure subsequent recognition or popularity. Readers of the 1960s and 1970s would have been more familiar with the goblins from George MacDonald's two princess tales, *The Princess and the Goblin* and *The Princess and Curdie,* as they would the phoenix and psammead from Nesbit's trilogy; and Frank Stockton's griffin from his *The Griffin and the Minor Canon,* while today's readers are more likely to know the magical beasts of the *Harry Potter* series.

3. Unicorns and Dragons

Unicorns and dragons are probably the best known of the mythical creatures in children's mixed fantasy. A unicorn assists Maria as she fights the evil Black Men of the forest in Elizabeth Goudge's *The Little White Horse*. Findhorn the Unicorn of Alan Garner's *Elidor* is rescued by children who are brought into Elidor for that purpose. Not only is Findhorn powerful—his death may have universe-wide repercussions—but, as legend stipulates, he is also obedient to a virgin, in this instance, young Helen. In C. S. Lewis's *The Last Battle,* he utilizes a unicorn, Jewel, whose prominence is evident since it is he who utters "Credo" when all the redeemed enter paradise. Gaudior the Unicorn, a major character in L'Engle's *A Swiftly Tilting Planet,* is sent to assist Charles Wallace's "going Within" so that the youth may prevent the breaking out of a worldwide nuclear war.

Dragons are perhaps more recognized and popular than unicorns, and fantasies these days appear to vie with one another in depicting dragons in different and novel ways. Kenneth Grahame enjoys the honor of first domesticating dragons in fiction in his *The Reluctant Dragon,* but in her *The Book of Dragons* Edith Nesbit showed for the first time, as she did so often, that dragons can appear effectively in various ways in children's fantasy. Blount states that, at least in Great Britain, dragons are usually not only domesticated but treated facetiously, such as C. S. Forester's *Poo Poo and the Dragons*, R. Weir's *Albert the Dragon*, and Margaret Mahy's *The Dragon of an Ordinary Family* (117). Dragons are also key characters with American writers. Ruth Stiles Gannett writes about them in *My Father's Dragon* and subsequent stories. A very recent humorous tale, Sarah Sargent's *Weird Henry Berg*, concerns a dragon who travels from Wales to Oshkosh, Wisconsin, to retrieve a baby dragon unexpectedly hatched from a dragon egg belonging to Henry Berg. More serious handling of dragons can be found in Lewis's *The Voyage of the Dawn Treader*, William Mayne's *A Game of Dark*, and Ursula Le Guin's *The Beginning Place* and Earthsea trilogy. Quite different is Jane Yolen's *Dragon's Blood*, a novel about the breeding and training of dragons for combat in the ring.

4. The Centaur and Dinosaur

Less popular by far than unicorns and dragons but nevertheless a striking addition to children's fantasy is the centaur. C. S. Lewis places the Centaur in Narnia as a representative of pagan time that merits redemption. More significant is the prominence given to centaurs by Robert Siegel's in *Alpha Centauri*. The surviving centaurs on Earth, a God-fearing and wise people, are rescued from possible extinction at the hands of their enemies, the Rock Movers, and helped to escape to Alpha Centauri, where they will live in a quasi-paradise.

The dinosaur, which today enjoys a kind of mythic and imaginative resurrection thanks to entertainment phenomena like the movie of Michael Crichton's *Jurassic Park* and the large purple TV character, "Barney," can be found (with some digging) in fairly early children's fantasy. A marble statue of a dinosaur graces the garden in Nesbit's *The Enchanted Castle* and briefly quickens into life. More recently, in Steve Senn's *The Double Disappearance of Walter Fozbel*, Walter one morning discovers that he has been transported to a world of dinosaurs in which human beings can be found only in museums, since they are extinct. With the help of some friendly dinosaurs, Walter barely manages to return to Earth and his normal existence.

5. *The Dress and Demeanor of Animals*

A familiar subtype of mixed fantasy is the story about talking animals who dress and behave as if they were civilized. Perhaps most well known are the animals of *The Wind in the Willows*, the various animals in *The Tale of Peter Rabbit* and the other Beatrix Potter tales, and the elephants, Babar, Celeste, Cornelius, and Arthur, in *Babar the Elephant* by Jean de Brunhoff. Fantasies about small animals, especially pets, definitely appeal to the special fondness that children harbor for creatures smaller than themselves. Examples abound: Hugh Lofting's *The Story of Doctor Dolittle*, despite its unfortunately racist depiction of Prince Bumpo, remains delightful and winning because of its portrait of Jip the dog, Dab-Dab the duck, Gub-Gub the pig, Polynesia the African parrot, Too-Too the owl, and Chee-Chee the monkey. *The Rescuers* and the other stories by Margery Sharp celebrate the exploits of Miss Bianca, Bernard, and the other members of the Mouse Prisoners' Aid Society. George Selden's classic *The Cricket in Times Square* and its sequel, *Tucker's Countryside*, is about the cricket, Chester, who sings operatic arias and brings pleasure to Mario and his family, and his friends, Harry Cat and Tucker Mouse. And Beverly Cleary's very popular *The Mouse and the Motorcycle* and its sequels, *Runaway Ralph* and *Ralph S. Mouse*, feature a mouse and his love affair with a motorcycle.

6. *Animals in Unique Roles*

The humanized animal story—such as, for instance, *Black Beauty* and Felix Salten's *Bambi*—attempt to guess at what is going on in the minds of animals. Edenic tales celebrate the idyllic lives animals supposedly can live without the presence of human beings, such as Dodie Smith's *The Hundred and One Dalmatians*, Walter de la Mare's *The Three Mulla-Mulgars*, and Tove Jansson's *Finn Family Moomintroll* and its various sequels about the Moomins and their home in Moominvalley. Lastly, there are the one-of-a-kind narratives, like Rudyard Kipling's *The Jungle Books*, which strives unsuccessfully to bridge the gap between human and animal; or the Narnian chronicles, with their original notion of fallen and redeemed animals; or Michael Bond's *A Bear Called Paddington* and its numerous successors that feature the little Peruvian bear who plays the role of an educated jester.

Magic Fantasy

There are some mixed fantasies that do not readily fit any of the sub-types already distinguished; hence, grouping these fantasies into their own subtype seems the only alternative. At first glance, this grouping looks like a makeshift arrangement, and the label of "magic fantasy" may seem to be too general. At second glances, however, magic fantasy as both subtype and name has merit. It does respect the integrity of the fantasies it covers. Moreover, it is quite appropriate, since magic is what accounts in the first place for these fantasies, and magic does play a key part in their plots. In any case, magic fantasy is mixed fantasy in which some unknown power impinges upon individuals and their affairs in ways that ordinarily are not manifested in the everyday world and that bring about unexpected results. For example, a bird-like boy suddenly appears in a village and teaches the children how to fly (Penelope Farmer's *The Summer Birds*); an old man gives an unhappy boy a bag of green crystals in order to ease his unhappiness, but the boy accidentally spills them near an old peach tree which, magically invigorated overnight, grows to an immense height and produces a gigantic peach (*James and the Giant Peach*, by Roald Dahl); a log entombing some un-known, mummified person mysteriously moves and follows a woman, apparently seeking vengeance for what happened centuries before (*The House on the Brink*, by John Gordon); an old woman instructs a young boy, whom she has selected as her successor, in the right uses of a pow-erful stone (*The Magic Stone*, by Leonie Kooiker); and placing favorite plastic toys into a mysterious cupboard and locking it with an old key, a family heirloom, not only transforms the toys into alive miniature people but also transports them into their own world where they are normal (*The Indian in the Cupboard*, by Lynne Reid Banks). Edith Nes-bit, it should be remembered, was the first children's fantasist to demonstrate that the impinging of magic upon the real world can be plausibly rendered and that the results of the intermingling may be se-rious as well as lighthearted, controlled as well as wild, and beneficent and supportive as well as malevolent and destructive.

Magic fantasy abounds in which the working of magic is light-hearted, although at times mischievous and irksome. For *Mary Poppins* Pamela Travers created a female protagonist with various skills, including flying, who, upon becoming a governess, turns the family she is working for topsy-turvy. Commander Pott in Ian Fleming's *Chitty-Chitty Bang Bang* lovingly rebuilds an old automobile that turns out to have a mind of its own as well as unexpected magic. In Penelope Lively's *The Revenge of Samuel Stokes*, an eighteenth-century landscape designer, put out by the threatened bulldozing of his masterpiece into a "total" housing project, attempts to flood out the entire housing tract, but Samuel Stokes is eventually placated, little permanent damage ensuing. A silver pencil, given Lizzy by her grandmother in Humphrey Carpenter's *The Captain Hook Affair*, enables the girl and her friends to bring to life with humorous results drawings based upon the illustrations in storybooks.

Fantasies depicting the serious results of magic's intervention in everyday life also abound. In Alexander's *The First Two Lives of Lukas-Kasha*, a "carnival joke" perpetrated by an illusionist—Lukas's placing his head into a bucket of water—transports the young man to a land where it was foretold that he would be king, and eventually he is. Just as abruptly as he entered the kingdom, Lukas is returned to his own time and world, having learned what it truly means to be one's self, especially when inspired by the adage "You can be what you imagine yourself to be." The Tuck family of Natalie Babbitt's *Tuck Everlasting*, while traveling one day through a wood, stop and drink at a spring that turns out to be a fountain of youth. The water and the fountain, readers are told, are all that remains from a previous ordering of affairs on Earth; except for this one place where a rent in the fabric separating magic from the real world still exists, all magic has been withdrawn from Earth. Because the Tucks' immortality is less than paradisiacal, the family works to prevent others from drinking the water and further interfering with the natural cycle of life. Perhaps because of her affectionate understanding of her elderly aunts, fourteen-year-old Clare, the protagonist of Penelope Lively's *The House in Norham Gardens*, finds her dreams haunted by New Guinea aborigines who are seeking the return of a particular tribal shield that the girl's great-grandfather took from the island decades earlier. Clare finds peace in her dreams and, at the same time, restores some dignity to the aborigines by presenting the shield to a museum for exhibit along with other artifacts of the natives. And in Manus Pinkwater's *Wingman*, high up on the George Washington Bridge, Wingman (a comic book hero who is Chinese) appears before Donald Chen. From the experience, the boy derives further pride in his race and trust in his talent for drawing.

A kind of magic fantasy currently enjoying readers' favor is the gothic novel. Strictly speaking, whether stories involving ghosts or incorporating witchcraft should be considered fantasy does depend upon the personal and social beliefs of readers, whether young or old. For instance, if some readers actually believe in the existence of ghosts and the possibility of witchcraft, then stories featuring ghosts or witches must be categorized as realistic fiction, even if in terms of plot and from a marketing perspective they are gothic fiction. On the other hand, if readers deny the existence of ghosts and refuse to take witchcraft seriously, these and similar stories are indeed fantasy. For the sake of this discussion, we have chosen to classify all gothic fiction as fantasy.

A few examples of gothic fiction that blend the supernatural with realism reveal the flavor of this subtype. In Patricia Clapp's *Jane-Emily*, Emily, a spoiled, embittered child while alive, seeks from the grave to take over Jane's body and mind so that the dead girl can retain control over her mother. John Bellairs's *The House with a Clock in Its Walls* tells a suspenseful story of two witches who plan to destroy the world but are thwarted by Lewis and his Uncle Jonathan. Janet Lunn's *Twin Spell* uses an old doll as the means whereby Hester returns after 120 years, seeking forgiveness for a horrible accident she apparently caused. Virginia Hamilton's *Sweet Whispers, Brother Rush* features a beguiling ghost who hangs around to set the record straight about his death and its implications for the family's welfare.

Children's fantasy, as a whole (with the possible exception of not-too-serious stories about ghosts and witches designed for Halloween seasonal reading), has not been very receptive to pure ghost stories, such as stories about some kind of reincarnation of a person who has definitely died. Sometimes, especially in time-slip stories, the dead who live again are not ghostly but depicted as if they are truly alive. For instance, in Nesbit's *The Story of the Amulet*, when the Queen of Babylon and the Egyptian priest, Rekh-mara, accidentally are brought forward to nineteenth-century England, they are flesh and blood, not wraiths. In Edward Ormondroyd's *Castaways on Long Ago*, Trelawny, the boy who had been drowned years ago, not only appears to Richard, Linda, and Dabley Waite in bodily form but is able to grasp a pencil in his hands and write messages—a task no mere vaporous ghost would be able to perform. Whether or not time travelers moving from the past into the present or vice versa are actually ghosts becomes a point of contention in Pearce's *Tom's Midnight Garden* when Tom and Hatty argue whether the boy or the girl may be a ghost trying to scare the other.

In another time-travel gothic adventure, Avi's *Devil's Race*, sixteen-year-old John Proud is caught in a struggle with the malevolent spirit of his great, great, great, great-grandfather and namesake, John Proud, who is looking for a new body to take over. Young John's uncle and cousin attempt to warn him about the dangers of the elder relative who has been hanged after being found guilty of being a demon. Seemingly going back in time, together they hike into the woods to visit the elder John Proud's grave, but Uncle Dave becomes sick and dies before he has the chance to tell young John something. The elder John Proud returns, this time on a crime spree, and invades young John's thoughts with a string of horrible consequences. Uncle Dave dies, Cousin Ann's parents are in a car accident, and Ann and John are forced to return to the trail to confront the evil relative. Eventually, the two John Prouds confront each other, and as he is encouraged to kill and hate, young John realizes that he must do the opposite. "Instantly, I leaped upon him. But instead of trying to kill him, I embraced him" (149). Symbolically, the two merge, acknowledging the inherent good and evil in all of us. Thematically, Avi has used elements of the heroic-ethical tradition with the struggle of good versus evil and coming of age. It is through love rather than hate that young John Proud faces his past, confronts the evil within, and triumphs.

Ghost Stories and Time-Slip Combinations

Although the gothic novel continues to hold great interest for many readers, it is important to note that the level of magic in this type of fantasy varies, and the presumed existence of ghosts, witchcraft, sorcery, and other supernatural entities is often key in understanding and solving the conflicts within the story. Sometimes the supernatural elements are the cause of the internal story crises, as found in the works of John Bellairs and Phyllis Reynolds Naylor. In other books the ghosts represent the supernatural in resolving a conflict, as seen in Pam Conrad's *Stonewords: A Ghost Story*, Betty Ren Wright's *Ghosts Beneath Our Feet* and *The Ghosts of Mercy Manor*, Virginia Hamilton's *Sweet Whispers, Brother Rush*, Avi's *Something Upstairs*, and Margaret Mahy's *The Changeover*. In all of these cases, however, the element of the supernatural is essential to the story, either as part of the problem or key in the solution.

Two notable creators of gothic fantasy who use the supernatural as essential elements of the plot structure and conflict are Phyllis Reynolds Naylor and John Bellairs. Both of these authors have created gothic fantasy for readers in the upper elementary to middle school reading levels. Their protagonists are young males and females of ten to thirteen years of age who focus on first identifying the evil witch or sorcerer who is causing the problem and then defeating or quashing the villain's destructive plans.

One popular author of gothic fantasy for young children is Phyllis Reynolds Naylor. Her series featuring Lynn Morley and her best friend Mouse and their battles against Mrs. Tuggle, a wicked witch who lives up the hill from Lynn and her family, are chilling accounts of the evil that black magic can render. Naylor's *Witch's Sister*, *The Witch's Eye*, *Witch Weed*, *Witch Water*, *The Witch Herself*, and *The Witch Returns* are a collection of adventures in which Lynn and Mouse attempt to uncover and thwart the evil plans of Mrs. Tuggle. Although the girls are convinced that Mrs. Tuggle is a witch, they are afraid to tell their parents or other adults too much for fear of its being dismissed as just "imaginative nonsense." So, throughout the first three books, Lynn and Mouse battle the evils of Mrs. Tuggle and attempt to keep her evil at bay without depending upon their parents for much support. Mouse's father has grown impatient with their talk of witchcraft, so the girls distance themselves from further adult discussions about their suspicions about Mrs. Tuggle. By the fourth book, however, the stakes begin to become too high for Lynn and Mouse when Lynn's mother comes under the influence of Mrs. Tuggle by renting space for a studio. As the story begins in *Witch Water*, Lynn reflects upon the connections that Mrs. Tuggle has over her family members.

> Mother, for instance, was a writer and had rented a remodeled hen house from the old woman to use as a studio. Judith, Lynn's sister had spent

most of her evenings last summer sewing with Mrs. Tuggle in an upstairs room of the ancient house. Stevie, Lynn's small brother, liked the stories Mrs. Tuggle told of bogles and hobyahs, and often wandered up to visit without telling anyone where he was going. And there was a pull deep inside Lynn herself that she couldn't explain. Perhaps it was this that frightened her most.

Lynn feels strongly that she needs proof that Mrs. Tuggle is a witch before bringing it up with her father or any adult again. But, over dinner one night, her father mentions the latest gossip circulating around the courthouse—that the death certificate for Mrs. Tuggle's brother, who supposedly drowned at age sixteen, is missing, leading to new questions of foul play. This bit of information sets Lynn and Mouse off on another adventure of intrigue and suspense as they set out to prove Mrs. Tuggle's connection to her brother's death or disappearance. No final answers are reached when the book ends; the reader is convinced that the mystery is not over.

In the fifth book, *The Witch Herself* , Naylor once again brings to the life the continuing saga of Lynn and Mouse and their attempt to reveal the true evils of Mrs. Tuggle. The story picks up exactly where *Witch Water* ends: "The crow was dead, but the cat was alive, and there was something very wrong." This bridge between the two books is so solid that one wonders if Naylor had planned *The Witch Herself* before finishing its predecessor. The text moves toward what seems to be the end for Mrs. Tuggle and her evil deeds. First, though, Lynn's family must live through some tough times. Her mother comes under the spell of Mrs. Tuggle when she moves her writing studio from the remodeled hen house to a room inside Mrs. Tuggle's home, because of an unusually cold winter, and subsequently suffers an increased level of anxiety and irritability. Ultimately, Lynn must risk her own life to save her mother when Mrs. Tuggle's house catches fire and is consumed, as is Mrs. Tuggle. Later, Lynn and Mouse visit the ruin of the house and find remains of the demonic cat chain and a glass eye that belonged to Mrs. Tuggle. As they realize their discovery among the ashes, the eye suddenly winks at them, ending the story on yet another possibility that the story of Mrs. Tuggle is not yet finished.

Phyllis Reynolds Naylor does indeed continue the story of Lynn, Mouse, and Mrs. Tuggle, the witch, but over a dozen years separates the publication of *The Witch Herself* (1978) and of *The Witch Returns* (1992). In the latter, final book of the series, Naylor does find an ending that puts closure on the evils of Mrs. Tuggle—not, however, without significant struggles for Lynn, Mouse, and their families.

In *The Witch Returns*, the reader discovers the reason behind Mrs. Tuggle's evilness, as well as the ultimate weapon against evil—love. The story unfolds as a house is being built on the site of Mrs. Tuggle's former home. The mystery begins to arise as the house takes on the identical design of Mrs. Tuggle's, right down to the detailing of the door knocker. Then, when Lynn and Mouse discover that it is Mrs. Tuggle's sister from England who is rebuilding—a sister that no one knew existed, who looks exactly like Mrs. Tuggle down to the same one green eye, one brown eye, and a gold tooth in the same spot—the tension begins to mount. What convinces the girls that Mrs. Tuggle has actually returned and not died in the fire is an anagram: "Elnora Tuggle" rearranged becomes the sister's name, Greta Gullone. The girls' fathers are also involved in the mystery. It remains difficult for Lynn and Mouse to proceed, because they are afraid that Lynn's mother will come under the influence of Mrs. Tuggle again. Thus begin the conflicts, suspicions, and distrust between family members that allow a space for Mrs. Tuggle's evil to surface again.

All of Naylor's work in this series parallels the work of John Bellairs in his three series. Both authors have produced stories of witchcraft, sorcery, and the supernatural to undergird certain universal themes of good versus evil. By creating stories in which particular key characters reappear and continue their struggles against evil, the reader can begin to see how characters grow and mature in their decision making while acknowledging that new temptations arise again and again, forcing the protagonists to rebattle and rethink their actions. Although other authors have created stories of witchcraft and sorcery, these two authors have successfully created series books that appeal to young readers while not submitting to the ease of predictable plots and conflicts.

John Bellairs was a prolific writer of gothic thrillers for young people and wrote some eighteen gothic novels for young people between 1973 and 1992, the year he died; three of them were published posthumously. His stories revolve around the adventures of three different male protagonists—Lewis Barnavelt, Johnny Dixon, and Anthony Monday—and weave the elements of a ghost story with sorcery, witchcraft, and the supernatural, creating a story fabric fraught with villains of the nether world.

Readers are often introduced to Bellairs's work through his first and probably best-known novel, *The House with a Clock in Its Walls* (1973). In this, the first of the series involving Lewis Barnavelt, his Uncle Jonathan, and neighbor Mrs. Zimmerman, the reader is introduced to Lewis, a ten-year-old boy who has lost both of his parents in a car accident and is on his way to live with an older uncle who lives in an old mansion in New Zebedee, Michigan. His uncle just happens to practice a little good magic as a sorcerer, as does his neighbor, Mrs. Zimmerman. None of this seems to be as problematic to Lewis as the ominous ticking heard within the walls of the house. And, although Uncle Jonathan has heard the ticking and suspects evil-doing (the original owner of the house was an evil sorcerer), he downplays the problem so as not to frighten his new houseguest. Lewis becomes involved with the mystery after he accidentally releases the dead spirit of the wicked wizard's wife into the present, where she begins the final work of her evil husband— to destroy the world. Ultimately, Lewis acts heroically by destroying the clock—an act that neither his Uncle Jonathan nor Mrs. Zimmerman was able to do.

This adventure, as with all the other adventures in this series, is set in the early 1950s and thus removed from present-day mores and lifestyles, suggesting to its readers that life in that time period was significantly different from today and lending to suspension of disbelief. The other four books in this series—*The Figure in the Shadows, The Letter, the Witch, and the Ring, The Ghost in the Mirror,* and *The Vengeance of the Witch-Finder*—all focus more heavily on the first novel's secondary characters, Mrs. Zimmerman and Rose Rita, neighbors and friends of Lewis. Within each of these gothic novels, however, the protagonist is faced with life-threatening (and sometimes soul-threatening) circumstances that require either Lewis or Rose Rita to fight the wicked witch or sorcerer for control, thereby stopping evil in its tracks.

It is apparent in these early books that Bellairs intended for his readers to see clear choices between good and evil and that good would always win out, albeit not without a tough fight. The ultimate choices are always clear, although often the protagonist is swayed during the process of the events to underestimate the power of evil.

A second series of gothic thrillers written by John Bellairs includes the young protagonist Anthony Monday and is set in the mid 1950s in Hoosac, Minnesota. His adventures involve his association with his older librarian friend, Miss Eells, and her brother, Emerson. This series consists of four books—*The Mansion in the Mist, The Treasure of Alpheus Winterborn, The Dark Secret of Weatherend,* and *The Lamp from the Warlock's Tomb*—in which, once again, the protagonist and his adult companions must solve the secrets that threaten to destroy the world and its order.

In *The Mansion in the Mist,* Anthony is spending a summer break with his elderly friends, Miss Eells and her brother Emerson, in Emerson's cabin in northern Canada. Although they're on vacation, they intend to find out why three previous renters of the cabin have disappeared. What they discover is a mysterious trunk that can (and does) transfer Anthony, Miss Eells, and Emerson to another world in which a deranged group is devising a plot to destroy the people of Earth. As with Bellairs's other works, the issues of good versus evil, with connections to witchcraft and sorcery, are manifold. Once again, we find an older person—in this case, Emerson—who is a dabbler in the magic arts and thus has the knowledge and background to help Anthony succeed in the netherworld adventures, ultimately destroying the forces of evil and rescuing his friends from death and destruction.

The third series written by John Bellairs is one in which the protagonist, Johnny Dixon, is again set in the early 1950s, this time in Gildersleeve, Massachusetts. In this series, Johnny's mother has died of cancer and his father is pilot in the Korean War, leaving Johnny to live with his grandparents, who are in their seventies. Johnny develops a friendship with the elderly gentleman who lives across the street—Professor Roderick Childermass—and Fergie, a classmate. As with the other Bellairs series, the older friend dabbles in the mysterious, often getting caught in supernatural adventures that thrust Johnny into precarious situations. This series, more often than the other two, places the protagonist and other innocent people at the mercy of evil-doers of the netherworld. Probably one of the most substantial differences between this series and the other works by Bellairs is the use of obvious satanic allusions. The villains that Johnny Dixon, Fergie, and Professor Childermass meet are often soul snatchers, un-

leashed by some seemingly innocent act by Johnny or his friends—
Professor Childermass, Dr. Coote, or Father Higgins.

In one of the first of this series, *The Mummy, the Will, and the Crypt*,
Johnny ignores Professor Childermass's advice to forget about the missing will of Mr. Glomus and the promised $10,000.00 reward, because
his grandmother is ill and needs surgery. His ignorance and determina-
tion to find the will place him in great danger, fighting what seems to
be supernatural forces that kill, mummify, and set the dead walking the
Earth. Not until Johnny is nearly killed does he realize that his search
was not necessary and that it was Mr. Glomus's sister who, connected
with evil forces, was the fiend behind the murders, mummies, and the
final destruction of the will.

In another early book in this series, *The Curse of the Blue Figurine*,
Johnny is curious about the mystery surrounding Father Bart and the
haunting of the church he built prior to the turn of the century. While
trying to avoid a bully who has been harassing him, Johnny wanders
around the basement of the church and unknowingly discovers a figurine that carries a warning not to remove it from the church premises.
Although he reads the warning, he does not heed it, and, when star-
tled, runs from the church with the figurine in his hands. That, when
coupled with a ring given him by a stranger, unleashes the evil spirit of
Father Bart, who though a priest, dabbled in the art of black magic,
probably selling his soul to the devil in the process. With this unleash-
ing of evil, Johnny must discover how to correct his deed without losing his own soul. Fortunately, with the help of Professor Childermass
and by sheer chance and luck, he is finally able destroy the evil spirit.

In yet another of Johnny Dixon's adventures in *The Spell of the Sorcerer's Skull*, Johnny unleashes the evil of a hanged sorcerer who at-
tempted to kill Professor Childermass's great-uncle when he picks up
the miniature skull that fell out of a haunted clock made by the professor's father years before. Once again, if falls to Johnny, with the help of
the professor, to correct Johnny's carelessness and rid the world of the
evil sorcerer once and for all—finally breaking the hex placed against
all of Professor Childermass's family.

In *The Trolley to Yesterday* published some five years later, in 1989,
Bellairs again creates a "spine tingling" (*Publisher's Weekly*) adventure
with Johnny and his friend Fergie, traveling with Professor Childermass

back in time via time machine to the Byzantine Empire as it readies for battle. The professor is trying the save the lives of some people hiding in a church, but he finally realizes that to fiddle with history could be disastrous to the future. While in Constantinople, however, they do find the inventor of the time machine and bring him back to the present— some thirty years after he left. Although there are no real demonic creatures present in this tale, there is magic and evil present threatening to hold the professor and the two boys in the past forever, much as Mr. Townsend, the inventor, was held for thirty years.

That same year, 1989, Bellairs had another Johnny Dixon mystery published—this one heavily laden with satanic overtones. In *The Chessman of Doom*, Johnny and his friend, Fergie, travel to Maine with Professor Childermass to spend the summer in the home of the professor's recently deceased brother, Peregrine. The professor's brother was quite eccentric and very wealthy and left his estate and moneys to the professor with the proviso that he live and care for the house without any paid help for the summer. Immediately upon their arrival, however, the three are caught up in the mystery of the Peregrine's death and apparent roaming spirit. As they delve into the mystery further, they find themselves caught up with an evil sorcerer who had deceived Peregrine and planned to destroy most of humankind instead of using the comet invention for peace. The spirit of Peregrine sends clues through riddles to his brother and ultimately, with a great deal of danger and risk, Childermass, his friend Dr. Coote, Johnny, and Fergie, with the help of "Crazy Annie" the witch, conquer the sorcerer, Mr. Stallybrass, who is then engulfed by the netherworld.

With the publication of *The Secret of the Underground Room* in 1990, Bellairs created another Johnny Dixon mystery of the supernatural involving Johnny, and Professor Childermass in the hunt for the professor's friend Father Higgins, who disappears after reporting that a ghost is trying to contact him. After traveling to England in search of Father Higgins, the professor, Johnny, and Fergie discover that Father Higgins's body has been taken over by an evil sorcerer who intends to release evil knights from the dead to wreak havoc upon the world. At the point in which the evil sorcerer is about finish the deed, Father Higgins's goodness emerges to destroy the treacherous plan. Although Johnny and Fergie are not directly responsible for either the problem or the solution of the case, they are both intimately involved in the location of the sorcerer and thus, of Father Higgins.

In addition to the eight books discussed above, John Bellairs wrote at least ten others involving the main characters of Lewis Barnavelt, Anthony Monday, or Johnny Dixon. He and Naylor are both notable for the success of their extensive gothic series. Meanwhile, a number of other authors have created a significant number of other gothic tales. Most recently, readers have enjoyed the exploits of Zoe in Pam Conrad's books, *Stonewords: A Ghost Story* and her sequel *Zoe Rising*. In the first book, Conrad tells the story of Zoe—a four-year-old girl who has gone to live with her grandparents because her mother is unable to care for her adequately or consistently. It is at this age that Zoe meets Zoe Louise—a ghost girl who lived in the house a hundred years before— and they become best friends. When they first meet, Zoe is younger than Zoe Louise by several years, but as Zoe grows older she begins to notice that Zoe Louise does not change and does not grow older. By the time Zoe is ten, she and Zoe Louise stand eye to eye, and from that time on, Zoe begins to see Zoe Louise as younger than herself. On one of the visits from Zoe's mother, they visit the old cemetery behind the house and her mother shows her the tombstones of the family who lived in the house years ago. On one tombstone is the "stoneword" of Zoe Louise and she realizes later that it must be the grave of her ghost friend, although she does not understand or know of her early death. As Zoe grows older, she begins to suspect that something happened. Searching through some old newspapers in her grandparents' basement, she discovers the fate of Zoe Louise. It then becomes her mission to change history and Zoe Louise's life.

The sequel to *Stonewords: A Ghost Story* picks up a year or two later, with Zoe as a fourteen-year-old going off to camp for the first time with a best friend, Jedidiah. In *Zoe Rising*, we find a young girl who realizes her fear of losing her grandparents when a fellow camper's parents are killed in an accident. Her sudden fear for her grandparents' well-being is so strong that she wills herself out of her body to find them. Throughout the story, Zoe runs into complications of trying to leave her body and travel across time and space without bringing suspicion upon herself and her friend Jedidiah. Since her behavior seems unusual and since she often returns with scratches or bruises, the camp personnel begin to watch her closely. Her will is so strong, however, that she defies them and continues to travel back in time to find her own mother as a child and ultimately rescues her from a kidnapper. Through time travel the mother and daughter are reunited at the end of the tale.

While both of these stories show Pam Conrad's flair for the gothic, the weaving of parallel plots lends originality to her works. Originality can be found also in works for young adults by Avi, Virgina Hamilton, Annette Curtis Klause, and Margaret Mahy. Within their texts, we often find similar themes of good versus evil, but often with a stronger twist of horror. These texts not only include ghosts, witches, and sorcerers but also can include such supernatural beings as vampires and werewolves.

In *The Changeover* by Margaret Mahy, fourteen-year-old Laura is aware that something is amiss when strange things begin to happen. Laura has experienced strange warnings before, first when her father left and more recently when a new student, Sorenson (Sorry) Carlisle, transferred to her school. Laura is convinced that Sorry is a witch and that no one knows but her. He is a good witch, however, and means no harm.

Helping to care for her three-year-old brother Jacko, Laura picks him up at the sitter's after school. On the way home, they stop at a new shop filled with all sorts of children's toys and curious items, but Laura immediately senses the danger. "Yet, once inside this enchanting shop, all Laura wanted was to get out again for it was full of the stale, sweet smell, laced with peppermint, that had assailed her in the morning—the smell of something very wrong and unable to conceal its wrongness" (23–24). Before they leave the shop, the owner, Carmody Braque, stamps young Jacko's hand, and the boy is at first delighted. Almost immediately, however, Jacko becomes disturbed about the stamp and pleads with his sister to remove it. "Take it off! This hand doesn't like it" (28). The stamp is of the actual face of Carmody Braque in such detail that it appeared three-dimensional. Laura tries to wipe it off but it won't budge. "It seemed to be *under* his skin, not on top of it, smiling, smiling, knowing it could not be touched by a mere handkerchief and the application of human spit" (28). Soon Jacko becomes very ill and modern medicine offers no solutions. Laura is forced to go to her classmate, Sorry Carlisle, and beg for the assistance of his witchcraft. She learns that Braque has chosen Jacko as his most recent life source and that Jacko will certainly die as Braque drains him of life. The only way she can rescue her brother is to become a witch herself and trick the storekeeper into letting her get close enough to put her stamp on him.

Laura agrees to the dangerous ceremony of the changeover. Dressed in white, she drinks wine mixed with a drop of her own blood. Armed with a sword and three stone coins, Laura is told that she must find her own way. She ventures into the forest and successfully completes her assignments. Together with her new friend, Sorry, she succeeds in killing the evil spirit of Braque and brings her brother back from the brink of death. Laura's mother has found a new mate, and life is going well. "Quite suddenly Laura knew what Sorry had once said was true. Like a holograph, every piece of the world contained the whole of the world if you stood at the right angle to it" (260). Real life was just as apt to contain magic as fairy tales if you were just willing to believe.

Blood and Chocolate, the second novel of Annnete Curtis Klause, is a gothic novel with an interesting twist. Teenage Vivian is in her junior year of high school and longs to fit in while hiding the oddity of her family and clan. "Blend in, she thought. If only I could" (11). How do you blend in when you're a werewolf? Vivian dates Alden, a human, and is intrigued by his culture. Adding to the obvious conflicts are the typical teenage problems. Her mother is too wild, and her siblings embarrass her. Additionally, Vivian is misunderstood at school, concerned with her appearance, and struggling to find her identity while feeling torn between two worlds.

This is a story of coming of age and of finding contentment in who you are. Vivian learns that there are beastlike qualities in all of us and that as a werewolf she has the ability to act on those instincts and purge them before they fester and turn evil.

> They can't change . . . But I do believe they have a beast within. In some it's buried so deep they'll never feel it; in others it stirs, and if a person can't give it a safe voice it warps and rots and breaks out in evil ways. They might not be able to change, but they still can be the beast of their own nightmares. It's our blessing that we can exorcise those demons. Sometimes it's our curse. (261)

This second book of Annette Curtis Klause is an interesting follow-up to her first gothic novel, *Silver Kiss*, a vampire love story. Her first novel also depicts a teenager who is fighting emotional battles of great proportion as her mother is dying of cancer. Klause appeals to the young adult reader who is looking for more than just a gothic horror novel.

In *Sweet Whispers, Brother Rush*, Virginia Hamilton introduces us to the protagonist Teresa and her ghost sighting in the very first paragraph of the novel.

> The first time Teresa saw Brother was the way she would think of him ever after. Tree fell head over heels for him. It was love at first sight in a wild being of her heart that took her breath. But it was a dark Friday three weeks later when it rained, hard and wicked, before she knew Brother Rush was a ghost. (9)

Brother Rush appears in her life at a time when her daily responsibilities seem to overwhelm her. Tree spends her time caring for her older brother Dab while her mother's job keeps her out of town. As Dab's illness progresses, Brother Rush comes to "take her out" and show her the events in her past that help to explain the present. She and her brother are able to go back in time through a mirror-like threshold on Brother Rush's palm. In her travels, she grows from infant to adult and experiences the events that constitute her prior life and explain her unanswered questions. Tree learns the details about her brother's illness and is forced to face his eventual death. In doing so, she learns how to step out of her immediate world and look back in. Brother Rush allows her the advantage of finding both the distance and the perspective to unite the fragments of her life and to find her place among them. Hamilton was one of the first to combine the supernatural with the adolescent problem novel, and in doing so sets both a precedent and a standard for others to follow.

Avi's *Something Upstairs* combines ghosts, time travel, and history in this well-crafted mystery. Kenny Huldorf, the protagonist, has recently moved from California to Rhode Island and is not entirely thrilled by the move. He is, however, pleased with his new room and private space on the third floor of their three-hundred-year-old home. When he steps into a small side room, he feels uneasy, hears a rustling sound, and notices a dark stain on the floor. "Certain that he heard something, Kenny turned back into the small room. The stain on the floor caught his eye again. As he looked at it, the thought came to him that it had something to do with a human death" (10). At loose ends with school not in session yet, Kenny becomes intrigued with the history of the house and begins his research in the public library.

At home, awakened by a noise, Kenny cautiously peers into the small side room and is astonished by what he sees.

> A white glow, almost shiny, and brightest on the floor, filled the windowless space. And what Kenny saw—or thought he saw—were two hands, then two arms, reaching up from the stain, pushing away a box of his mother's old books that was sitting on it. These hands and arms seemed to be not flesh and blood but sculptured, glowing smoke. It was as if, from under that box, a body was struggling to be free. (14)

The ghost Kenny meets is that of Caleb, a young boy who had been a slave of a previous owner of the house. Kenny discovers that the stain on the floor is blood from Caleb's murder. Caleb explains that he is destined to appear to each new owner to ask assistance in discovering and stopping his murderer and so averting his death. Only when his murder is solved will Caleb be free to leave the house.

With some hesitation, Kenny agrees to help Caleb and travels back in time to solve the mystery. Together the two boys trick the would-be murderer and instead murder him, thereby freeing Caleb and altering history.

Bellairs, Naylor, Conrad, Avi, Hamilton, Klause, Mahy, and others have all contributed to a genre that continues to grow. The popularity of ghost stories, time travel, and tales of the supernatural delight young readers and reinforce the universal theme of good versus evil at every level.

Conclusions

Mixed fantasy remains one of the most popular forms of literature for young people. Time travel, transformation, talking animals and toys, and magic feed our human need to experience the unknown through the joining of the real and unreal universes. By doing so, we, as readers, are freed from the confines of the here and now and allowed to enter the world of genuinely imaginative literature.

Works Cited and Other Titles Mentioned

Adams, Richard. *Watership Down*. New York: Macmillan, 1974.

Alexander, Lloyd. *The Book of Three*. New York: Holt, 1964.

———. *The First Two Lives of Lukas-Kasha*. New York: Dutton, 1978.

———. *Time Cat*. New York: Puffin, 1963.

Andersen, Hans Christian. "The Ugly Duckling." In *Fairytales*. New York: Grosset & Dunlap, 1945.

Anderson, Margaret J. *In the Circle of Time*. New York: Knopf, 1979.

Avi. *Devil's Race*. New York: Harper Collins, 1984.

———. *Perloo the Bold*. New York: Scholastic, 1998.

———. *Poppy*. Illus. Brian Floca. New York: Avon, 1995.

———. *Poppy and Rye*. Illus. Brian Floca. New York: Avon, 1998.

———. *Something Upstairs*. New York: Avon, 1988.

Babbitt, Natalie. *Tuck Everlasting*. New York: Farrar, Straus & Giroux, 1975.

Bailey, Carolyn. *Miss Hickory*. New York: Viking, 1946.

Banks, Lynne Reid. *The Indian in the Cupboard*. New York: Doubleday, 1982.

———. *Return of the Indian*. New York: Bantam/Doubleday, 1986.

Barrie, James Matthew. *Peter Pan*. 1911. New York: Bantam, 1985.

Baum, I. Frank. *The Wonderful Wizard of Oz*. Chicago: Reilly & Lee, 1956.

Bellairs, John. *The Chessmen of Doom*. New York: Dial, 1989.

———. *The Curse of the Blue Figurine*. New York: Dial, 1983.

———. *The Drum, the Doll, and the Zombie*. New York: Dial, 1994.

———. *The Figure in the Shadows*. New York: Dial, 1975.

———. *The Ghost in the Mirror*. New York: Dial, 1993.

———. *The House with a Clock in Its Walls*. New York. Dial, 1973.

———. *The Letter, the Witch, and the Ring*. New York: Dial, 1976.

———. *The Mansion in the Mist*. New York: Puffin, 1992.

———. *The Mummy, the Will, and the Crypt*. New York: Dial, 1983.

———. *The Secret of the Underground Room*. New York: Dial 1990.

———. *The Spell of the Sorcerer's Skull*. New York: Dial, 1984.

———. *The Trolley to Yesterday*. New York: Dial, 1989.

Berton, Pierre. *The Secret World of Og*. Boston: Little, Brown, 1962.

Blount, Margaret. *Animal Land: The Creatures of Children's Fiction*. New York: Avon, 1977.

Bond, Michael. *A Bear Called Paddington*. New York: Houghton, 1960.

Bond, Nancy. *A String in the Harp*. New York: Atheneum, 1976.

Boston, Lucy. *The Children of Green Knowe*. New York: Harcourt, 1967.

———. *The River at Green Knowe*. New York: Harcourt, 1959.

Brooks, Walter R. *Freddy and the Baseball Team from Mars*. New York: Knopf, 1955.

Burman, Ben Lucien. *Seven Stars for Catfish Bend*. New York: Avon, 1977.

Carpenter, Humphrey. *The Captain Hook Affair*. Harmondsworth, UK: Puffin, 1982.

Carroll, Lewis. *Alice in Wonderland,* 1865.

Cassedy, Syliva. *Beyond the Attic Wall*. New York: Avon, 1983.

Clapp, Patricia. *Jane-Emily*. New York: Lothrop, Lee, 1969.

Clarke, Pauline. *The Return of the Twelves*. New York: Morrow, 1965.

Cleary, Beverly. *The Mouse and the Motorcycle*. New York: Morrow, 1965.

———. *Ralph S. Mouse*. New York: Morrow, 1982.

———. *Runaway Ralph*. New York: Morrow, 1970.

Collodi, Carlo. *Pinocchio*. New York: Macmillan, 1969.

Conrad, Pam. *Stonewords: A Ghost Story*. New York: HarperCollins, 1990.

Coombs, Patricia. *Lisa and the Grompet*. New York: Dell, 1980.

Cooney, Caroline B. *Both Sides of Time*. New York: Bantam, 1995.

Cross, John Kier [Stephen MacFarlane]. *The Other Side of Green Hills*. New York: Coward, 1947.

Curry, Jane Louise. *The Mysterious Shrinking House*. New York: Scholastic, 1965.

———. *The Sleepers*. New York: Harcourt, 1968.

Dahl, Roald. *James and the Giant Peach*. New York: Knopf, 1961.

———. *The Magic Finger*. New York: Harper, 1966.

Dann, Colin. *The Animals of Farthing Wood*. London: Pan, 1980.

Davidson, Lionel. *Under Plum Lake*. New York: Knopf, 1980.

De Brunhoff, Jean. *Babar the Elephant*. New York: Random House, 1937.

De La Mare, Walter. *The Three Mulla-Mulgars*. New York: Knopf, 1919.

Duncan, Lois. *Stranger with My Face*. New York: Little, Brown, 1981.

———. *Summer of Fear*. New York: Little, Brown, 1976.

Eager, Edward. *Half Magic*. New York: Harcourt, 1954.

———. *Seven Day Magic*. New York: Harcourt, 1962.

Farmer, Penelope. *A Castle of Bone*. New York: Atheneum, 1972.

———. *The Summer Birds*. New York: Harcourt, 1962.

Field, Rachel. *Hitty: Her First Hundred Years*. New York: Macmillan 1937.

Fisk, Pauline. *Midnight Blue*. Batavia, Ill.: Lion, 1990.

Fleming, Ian. *Chitty-Chitty Bang Bang*. New York: Random House, 1964.

Forester, C. S. *Poo Poo and the Dragons*. Boston: Little, Brown, 1942.

Gannett, Ruth Stiles. *My Father's Dragon*. New York: Random House, 1948.

Garner, Alan. *Elidor*. New York: Walck, 1965.

———. *The Moon of Gomrath*. New York: Walck, 1967.

———. *Red Shift*. New York: Macmillan, 1973.

———. *The Weirdstone of Brisingamen*. New York: Walck, 1968.

George, Jean Craighead. *Julie of the Wolves*. New York: Harper & Row, 1972.

Gordon, John. *The House on the Brink*. New York: HarperCollins, 1971.

Goudge, Elizabeth. *The Little White Horse*. New York: Coward, 1946.

Grahame, Kenneth. *The Reluctant Dragon*. New York: Holiday, 1953.

———. *The Wind in the Willows*. New York: Scribner, 1933.

Hahn, Mary Downing. *Time for Andrew: A Ghost Story*. New York: Avon, 1994.

———. *Time of the Witch*. New York: Clarion, 1982.

Hamilton, Virginia. *Sweet Whispers, Brother Rush*. New York: Philomel, 1982.

Hoban, Russell. *The Mouse and His Child*. New York: Harper, 1967.

Jansson, Tove. *Finn Family Moomintroll*. New York: Avon, 1975.

Jarrell, Randall. *The Animal Family*. New York: Pantheon, 1965.

Juster, Norton. *The Phantom Tollbooth*. New York: Random House, 1961.

Kendall, Carol. *The Gammage Cup*. New York: Harcourt, 1959.

Kingsley, Charles. *The Water-Babies*. New York: Doubleday, 1954.

Kipling, Rudyard. *The Jungle Books*. New York: Dell, 1964.

Klause, Annette Curtis. *Blood and Chocolate*. New York: Delacorte, 1997.

———. *The Silver Kiss*. New York: Delacorte, 1990.

Kooiker, Leonie. *The Magic Stone*. New York: Morrow, 1978.

Langton, Jane. *The Astonishing Stereoscope*. New York: Harper, 1971.

———. *The Diamond in the Window*. New York: Harper, 1962.

———. *The Fledgling*. New York: Harper, 1980.

———. *The Swing in the Summerhouse*. New York: Harper, 1967.

Lawson, Robert. *Rabbit Hill*. New York: Viking, 1944.

Le Guin, Ursula. *The Beginning Place*. New York: Harper, 1980.

———. *The Farthest Shore*. New York: Atheneum, 1972.

———. *Tehanu: The Last Book of Earthsea*. New York: Macmillan, 1990

———. *The Tombs of Atuan*. New York: Atheneum, 1971.

———. *A Wizard of Earthsea*. New York: Bantam, 1975.

Lemon, Mark. *The Enchanted Doll and Tinykin's Transformations*. New York: Garland, 1976.

L'Engle, Madeleine. *An Acceptable Time*. New York: Dell, 1989.

———. *Many Waters*. New York: Farrar, Straus & Giroux, 1986.

———. *A Swiftly Tilting Planet*. New York: Farrar, Straus & Giroux, 1978.

———. *A Wind in the Door*. New York: Farrar & Strauss & Giroux, 1973.

———. *A Wrinkle in Time*. New York: Farrar, Stauss & Giroux, 1962.

Lewis, C. S. *The Last Battle*. New York: Macmillan, 1956.

———. *The Lion, the Witch, and the Wardrobe*. New York: Macmillan, 1951.

———. *The Magician's Nephew*. New York: Macmillan, 1970.

———. *The Voyage of the Dawn Treader*. New York: Macmillan, 1952.

Linklater, Eric. *The Gold Dust Letters*. New York: Orchard Books, 1994.

———. *The Wind on the Moon*. New York: Macmillan, 1944.

Lively, Penelope. *The House in Norham Gardens*. New York: Dutton, 1974.

———. *The Revenge of Samuel Stokes*. New York: Dutton, 1981.

———. *A Stitch in Time*. New York: Dutton, 1976.

———. *The Whispering Knights*. New York: Dutton, 1976.

Lobel, Arnold. *Fables*. New York: Harper, 1980.

Lofting, Hugh. *The Story of Doctor Dolittle*. New York: Lippincott, 1920.

Lunn, Janet. *The Root Cellar*. New York: Scribner, 1983.

———. *Twin Spell*. New York: Harper, 1969.

McCaffery, Anne. *Dragondrums*. New York: Atheneum, 1979.

———. *Dragonsong*. New York: Atheneum, 1976.

———. *Dragonstar*. New York: Atheneum, 1977.

———. *Moreta: Dragon Lady of Pern*. New York: Ballantine, 1983.

———. *The White Dragon*. New York: Ballantine, 1978.

MacDonald, George. *At the Back of the North Wind*. New York: Macmillan, 1964.

———. *The Princess and Curdie*. New York: Macmillan, 1945.

———. *The Princess and the Goblin*. New York: Penguin, 1964.

McHargue, Georgess. *Stoneflight*. New York: Viking, 1975.

Mahy, Margaret. *The Changeover*. New York: Atheneum, 1984.

———. *Dangerous Spaces*. New York: Puffin, 1991.

———. *The Haunting*. New York: Atheneum, 1982.

———. *The Tricksters*. New York: McElderry, 1987.

Major, Kevin. *Blood Red Ochre*. New York: Delacorte, 1989.

Mayne, William. *Earthfasts*. New York: Dutton, 1967.

———. *A Game of Dark*. New York: Dutton, 1971.

Mikolaycak, Charles. *Babushka*. New York: Holiday House, 1984.

Molesworth, Mary. *The Cuckoo Clock*. New York: Dutton, 1954.

———. *The Tapestry Room*. New York: Dutton, 1954.

Naylor, Phyllis, Reynolds. *The Witch Herself*. New York: Dell, 1978.

———. *The Witch Returns*. New York: Dell, 1992.

———. *Witch Water*. New York: Dell, 1977.

Nesbit, Edith. *The Book of Dragons*. New York: Looking Glass (n.d.).

———. *The Children and It*. New York: Penguin, 1959.

———. *The Enchanted Castle*. New York: Dent, 1968.

———. *The Phoenix and the Carpet*. New York: Penguin, 1959.

———. *The Story of the Amulet*. New York: Penguin, 1959.

Nichols, Beverley. *The Stream That Stood Still*. London: Fontana, 1975.

———. *The Tree That Sat Down*. London: Fontana, 1975.

Nichols, Ruth. *The Marrow of the World*. New York: Atheneum, 1972.

Nixon, Joan Lowry. *Whispers from the Dead*. New York: Delacorte, 1989.

Norton, Andre. *Fur Magic*. New York: Archway, 1978.

———. *Quag Keep*. New York: Atheneum, 1978.

———. *Steel Magic*. New York: Archway, 1978.

Norton, Mary. *The Borrowers*. New York: Harcourt, 1953.

O'Brien, Robert C. *Mrs. Frisbie and the Rats of NIMH*. New York: Atheneum, 1971.

Ormondroyd, Edward. *All in Good Time*. New York: Parnassus, 1975.

———. *Castaways on Long Ago*. New York: Parnassus, 1973.

———. *Time at the Top*. New York: Parnassus, 1963.

Park, Ruth. *Playing Beatie Bow*. New York: Atheneum, 1982.

Pearce, Philippa. *Tom's Midnight Garden*. New York: Lippincott, 1959.

Peck, Richard. *The Ghost Belonged to Me*. New York: Viking 1975.

———. *Ghosts I Have Been*. New York: Viking, 1977.

———. *Voices after Midnight*. New York: Delacorte, 1989.

Pierce, Meredith Ann. *The Darkangel Trilogy. The Pearl of the Soul of the World*. New York: Little, Brown, 1990.

Pinkwater, D. Manus. *Wingman*. New York: Dodd, 1975.

Potter, Beatrix. *The Tale of Peter Rabbit*. London: Frederick Warne, 1902.

Proysen, Alf. *Mrs. Pepperpot to the Rescue*. New York: Pantheon, 1964.

Pullman, Philip. *The Ruby Smoke*. New York: Random House, 1985.

———. *Shadow in the North*. New York: Knopf, 1986.

———. *The Tiger in the Well*. New York: Random House, 1990.

Rowling, J. K. *Harry Potter and the Chamber of Secrets*. New York: Scholastic, 1999

———. *Harry Potter and the Goblet of Fire*. New York: Scholastic, 2000

———. *Harry Potter and the Prisoner of Azkaban*. New York: Scholastic, 1999.

———. *Harry Potter and the Sorcerer's Stone*. New York: Scholastic, 1998.

Salten, Felix. *Bambi*. New York: Simon & Schuster, 1928.

Sargent, Sarah. *Weird Henry Berg*. New York: Crown, 1980.

Sauer, Julia. *Fog Magic*. New York: Viking, 1943.

Selden, George. *The Cricket in Times Square*. New York: Farrar, Straus & Giroux, 1960.

———. *Tucker's Countryside*. New York: Farrar, Straus & Giroux, 1969.

Senn, Steve. *The Double Disappearance of Walter Fozbek*. New York: Hastings House, 1980.

Service, Pamela F. *The Reluctant God*. New York: Ballantine, 1988.

Sewell, Anna. *Black Beauty*. New York: H. M. Caldwell, 1894.

Sharp, Margery. *The Rescuers*. Boston: Little, Brown, 1959.

Sherburne, Zoa. *Why Have the Birds Stopped Singing?* New York: Morrow, 1974.

Siegel, Robert. *Alpha Centauri*. Westchester, Ill.: Cornerstone Books, 1980.

Smith, Dodie. *The Hundred and One Dalmations*. New York: Viking, 1957.

Snyder, Zilpha Keatley. *Black and Blue Magic*. New York: Atheneum, 1972.

Steele, Mary Q. *Journey Outside*. New York: Viking, 1969.

Stewart, Mary. *A Walk in Wolf Wood*. New York: Morrow, 1980.

Stockton, Frank. *The Griffin and the Minor Canon*. New York: Holt, 1963.

Thurber, James. *Many Moons*. New York: Harcourt, 1943.

———. *The 13 Clocks*. Illus. Marc Simont. New York: Dell, 1990 (reprint).

Travers, Pamela. *Mary Poppins*. New York: Harcourt, 1962.

Uttley, Alison. *A Traveler in Time*. New York: Viking, 1940.

Waugh, Sylvia. *Mennyms*. New York: Avon, 1993.

Weir, Rosemary. *Albert the Dragon*. New York: Abelard-Schuman, 1961.

White, E. B. *Charlotte's Web*. New York: Harper, 1952.

———. *Stuart Little*. New York: Harper, 1945.

White, T. H. *The Sword in the Stone*. New York: Dell, 1973.

Williams, Jay. *The Hero from Otherwhere*. New York: Walck, 1972.

Williams (Bianco), Margery. *The Velveteen Rabbit*. New York: Doubleday, 1958.

Wiseman, David. *Jeremy Visick*. Boston: Houghton Mifflin, 1981.

Wrede, Patricia C. *Calling on Dragons*. New York: Harcourt Brace Jovanovich, 1990.

———. *Dealing with Dragons*. New York: Harcourt Brace Jovanovich, 1990.

———. *Searching for Dragons*. New York: Harcourt Brace Jovanovich, 1991.

———. *Talking to Dragons*. New York: Harcourt Brace Jovanovich, 1985.

Wright, Betty Ren. *Ghosts Beneath Our Feet*. New York: Scholastic, 1984.

———. *The Ghosts of Mercy Manor*. New York: Scholastic, 1993.

Yep, Laurence. *Dragon Cauldron*. New York: HarperCollins, 1991.

———. *Dragon of the Lost Sea*. New York: HarperCollins, 1982.

———. *Dragon War*. New York: HarperCollins, 1992.

———. *Dragonwings*. New York: HarperCollins, 1975.

———. *Sweetwater*. New York: Harper, 1973.

Yolen, Jane. *The Devil's Arithmetic*. New York: Penguin, 1988.

———. *Dragon's Blood*. New York: Delacorte, 1982.

Zipes, Jack, ed. *The Outspoken Princess and the Gentle Knight*. Illus. Stephane Poulin. New York: Bantam, 1994.

CHAPTER FOUR

~

Heroic-Ethical Traditions

The most rewarding and at the same time most challenging of children's fantasy may be the heroic-ethical. In part, the challenge results from its engrossing and stimulating subject matter and theme and also from its relatively high literary quality. One thinks, for instance, of C. S. Lewis's Narnian chronicles, Alexander's Prydain chronicles, Tolkien's *The Hobbit*, Susan Cooper's *The Dark Is Rising* sequence, Ursula K. Le Guin's Earthsea trilogy, Alan Garner's Brisingamen novels, L'Engle's *A Wrinkle in Time*, Philip Pullman's *Golden Compass*, and J. K. Rowling's *Harry Potter* series. All of them have been honored in one way or another, some even with the Newbery Medal, the National Book Award, Best Book of the Year in English, or American Library Association Notable.

To label this subtype of fantasy as heroic-ethical instead of heroic or high (as has been customary), or ethical (as has been suggested recently) is, frankly, a compromise, conceding that the various titles making up the subtype can be usefully approached in two somewhat different ways, depending upon an individual's preference or purpose. If one stresses plot, characterization, and style, then "heroic" or "high"—the two terms are interchangeable—may be a more accurate designation; on the other hand, if one wishes to emphasize the author's intention, subject matter, or possible effects upon the readers, then "ethical" may be preferable. Further, in view of the fact that many titles appear under both subtypes, "heroic-ethical" after all may be as accurate a designation as one can hope for.

Definitions

Much of what has been called heroic or high fantasy, whether for children or adults, is an adaptation of traditional heroic or mythic conventions and material that presupposes a world, as Northrop Frye puts it, "of heroes and gods and titans . . . a world of powers and passions and moments of ecstasy far greater than anything we meet outside the imagination" (100). It goes without saying that children's and young adult heroic-ethical fantasy, when it involves adaptation of traditional material, must do so in ways comprehensible or attractive to young readers. The nature of the heroism dramatized must have the potential for satisfying the young readers' dream of significant competence and self-worth. Eleanor Cameron, the well-known critic and author of children's books (including heroic-ethical fantasy), when speaking of heroic or high fantasy, stresses the influence it can have on young readers: "For within these tales lies the essence of their creators, the philosophy of their lives subtly woven which may, quite unbeknown to the children themselves, become a lasting influence" (130). Also helpful in understanding heroic-ethical fantasy are some of the remarks of Marshall Tymm, Kenneth Zahorski, and Robert Boyer in the introduction to *Fantasy Literature: A Core Collection and Reference Guide*, especially the distinction between high—the term they prefer over heroic—and low fantasy.

> . . . the world of low fantasy is the primary world—this real world we live in. It too demonstrates a consistent order, but its order is explainable in terms of natural law (which excludes the supernatural and the magical—for the most part). The gods and faeries no longer, alas, walk here. Consequently, when something nonrational occurs, as it does in low fantasies such as Peter S. Beagle's *Lila the Werewolf* and Oscar Wilde's *Portrait of Dorian Gray*, there are no explanations, rational or non-rational. The causes simply are not forthcoming: they are inexplicable. In a high fantasy secondary world, the metamorphosis of a young lady into a wolf or the aging of the portrait of Dorian Gray would be ex-

plained by some magical or supernatural agency that would be accepted in that world. (5)

A central, though not essential, mark of heroic or high fantasy, then, is the presence of a secondary world in which nonrational causality operates.

A secondary world, Tymm et al. point out, can relate to the primary world in three ways (5–6). First, a particular fantasy opens within a secondary world and remains there, the primary world simply ignored. Having no visible connection to Earth, both Tolkien's Middle Earth and Le Guin's Earthsea exist independent of it. Alexander's Prydain enjoys the same kind of independence even if it may vaguely resemble Wales. In a second variant, some kind of direct relationship between the two worlds is set up, perhaps because a comparison or contrast between them may heighten readers' sense of wonder at the distinctiveness of the secondary world. One familiar and still striking instance occurs in the film *The Wizard of Oz*. After Dorothy is knocked unconscious in her bedroom and the entire house is carried away by the cyclone—scenes shot in black and white—she awakens and, not knowing where she is, opens the door; suddenly, as Dorothy and viewers are introduced to Oz, the entire screen fills with color. Victor Fleming, the director of the film, brilliantly took advantage of the nature of film to heighten vividly the contrast between Kansas and Oz.

The same scene in both book and film illustrates another aspect of the second kind of relationship that can exist between the primary and secondary worlds. Between the two, often there is a portal, rent, or transfer point, and its functions, as has been discussed already, need to be described or rationalized. Accordingly, in the book *The Wizard of Oz* a cyclone transports Dorothy from Kansas to Oz and, it will be recalled, the magic of her silver shoes enables the girl to return home.

A third kind of secondary world exists within the primary world or its magical power is manifest at a very restricted location within the primary world. Only during midsummer's night on the grounds of the castle bathed in moonlight can the world of classical beauty materialize in Nesbit's *The Enchanted Castle*. In William Mayne's *Earthfasts* the meadowland undulates and opens up, and out marches an eighteenth-century British grenadier magically awakened not from death but from sleep. In Jane Louise Curry's *The Sleepers*, a cave magically secures the sleeping King Arthur and his knights, who wait until Great Britain needs their assistance. And in Diana Wynne Jones's *Power of Three*, magic seals the doors and gates of the mounds and caverns of the Lymen and Dorig so that the Giants (human beings residing on the Berkshire Moor) cannot see them.

According to Tymm et al., nonrational events occur in low fantasy without causality or explanation and can generate humor or horror, depending on the kind of story, but not awe or wonder, which are more characteristic of high or heroic fantasy, which usually plays out in secondary worlds. Moreover, awe and wonder are effectively reinforced by three distinctive features in high fantasy: noble characters, archetypes, and elevated style. Characters are made noble because of high birth or class or because they are capable of performing noble deeds. Archetypes—basic symbols or configurations like the shadow, an old woman, or a tree—are often found in high fantasy; readers' recognition of archetypes accounts for much of the appeal and satisfaction of reading fantasy. The characteristic "elevated" language of high fantasy is evocative, sometimes quite formal, and artificial—language that Tymm et al. believe helps readers to feel wonder and awe. These three features of nobility, archetypes, and elegant style are usually absent from low fantasy, and whatever awe and wonder may lie in a low-fantasy plot usually lacks the benefit of their support.

What is ethical fantasy, the other component of the heroic-ethical? A sprawling subcategory, it cuts across various subtypes of children's and young adult fantasy, including what others call heroic or high. Concerned not so much with form but with distinctive subject matter, specific intent, and purpose, ethical fantasy has been described as:

> explicitly concerned with the existence of good and evil and the morality of human behavior. Neither technical nor argumentative, ethical fantasy takes for granted that good and evil exist and that there are substantive, discernible differences between them. At the same time it concedes that the differences are not always easily discernible. Actually, the plots of ethical fantasy often focus on the difficulty and, sometimes, even the necessity of discerning right from wrong and then of acting accordingly. Also, ethical fantasy presumes that the choices and decisions of

young people, whether they are fully aware or not, involve taking sides between good and evil and sometimes may have results different from what the individual intends or foresees. Further, ethical fantasy presumes that choosing between right and wrong and accepting the consequences of that choice are marks of maturity. In ethical fantasy, then, making moral decisions is an important plot element. (Molson, 86–87)

Patterns in Heroic-Ethical Fantasy

Basic to heroic-ethical fantasy is the presence of young protagonists. There are Peter, Susan, Lucy, and Edmund Pevensie in the first three of Lewis's Narnian chronicles; Taran in Alexander's Prydain chronicles; Simon, Jane, and Barney Drew and Will Stanton and Bran Davies in Cooper's *The Dark Is Rising* sequence; Meg and Charles Wallace in L'Engle's time trilogy; Fiona and Bran McCool in Mary Tannen's *The Wizard Children of Finn* and its sequel, *The Lost Legend of Finn*; Becky in Siegel's *Alpha Centauri*; Lewis in Bellairs's *The House with a Clock in Its Walls*; Nita and Kit in Diane Duane's *Wizardry Series*, to mention a few. Often, the protagonists are not children but still are sufficiently childlike in physical appearance and behavior that young people can readily identify with them. Consider Bilbo of Tolkien's *The Hobbit*, for instance, or the Minnipin heroes, Gummy, Curley Green, Walter the Earl, Muggies, and Mingy, in Carol Kendall's *The Gammage Cup*.

Although the presence of young protagonists in heroic-ethical fantasy may be obvious and taken for granted, its significance may not be fully appreciated. The centrality of children and young people in heroic-ethical fantasy signals that its authors in all likelihood not only have in mind young readers as their prime audience but seek deliberately to capitalize on youth's strong desire to identify with what they read. The kind of identification that heroic-ethical fantasy offers is sophisticated and similar to what D. W. Harding discusses in his analysis of what transpires in the reading process.

> Wish-fulfillment in novels and plays can . . . be described as wish-formulation or the definition of desires. . . . It is the social act of affirming with the author a set of values. . . . [F]ictions contribute to defining the reader's values.

> Empathic insight allows the spectator to view ways of life beyond
> his own range . . . he can achieve an imaginary development of hu-
> man potentialities that have remained rudimentary in himself . . . The
> spectator enters imaginatively . . . into some of the multifarious pos-
> sibilities that he has not himself been able to achieve. (Harding,
> 69–70)

Two of Harding's remarks are especially useful. One is that empathic
insight or identification allows readers the means to try on or try out
a variety of roles and options that are out of their current range or
circumstances. The other is that the term "wish-formulation" or
value formulation is both a more accurate and positive term than
"wish-fulfillment," the term more commonly misused by those seeking to disparage fantasy. With Harding's help, then, one can understand better the ways heroic-ethical fantasy fosters identification
that can be empathic and supportive. For one, heroic-ethical fantasy,
once it has had an opportunity to work its magic, beckons young
readers to examine their own fantasies, dreams, hopes of achievement, public acknowledgment, and praise, recognizing them for
what they actually are: evidence of the readers' genuine capability
and enthusiastic willingness to test new options once they materialize. Moreover, heroic-ethical fantasy reinforces young peoples' conviction that it is indeed worthwhile to create and test new options
and that the resulting high self-esteem is real or readily obtainable.
Finally, heroic-ethical fantasy assures readers that there is no call for
them to be embarrassed by their specific fantasies, dreams, and
hopes, because other young people cherish similar ones.

Heroic-ethical fantasy readily facilitates the readers' empathic identification because of the various kinds of situations in which protagonists are placed. The impulsive mischief of young Digoryu's tapping a
bell he was not supposed to in Lewis's *The Magician's Nephew* awakens
Jadis, the wicked Empress, collapses a major temple, and culminates in
the introduction of evil into the newly created, innocent Narnia. A
young boy, Taran, by mindlessly chasing after the runaway pig, Hen
Wen, in Alexander's *The Book of Three* sets into motion a sequence
that ultimately brings about, four volumes later in *The High King*, the
destruction of Arawn-Death-Lord and the emergence of the long

promised High King who brings peace to Prydain. By deciphering codes, watching over and reading maps, finding lost items, and just being available, Simon, Barney, and Jane play essential roles in Cooper's *The Dark Is Rising* series. Jane, in particular, through her openly avowed sympathy for the Greenwitch, induces the latter in *Greenwitch* to return to the Masters of Light an important document that they need to secure the ultimate victory over the Dark. When Martha, Susie, and William in Penelope Lively's *The Whispering Knights* ask Miss Hepplewhite if they may help in the old woman's struggle against the "bad side of things," she replies that the children definitely are not useless.

> "What can we do?" asked William. "I mean, we're not much, are we? Compared to her. Three children."
> "It doesn't matter what you look like or who you are. It's courage and conviction that count," said Miss Hepplewhite. (chapter 4)

Regardless of how any heroic-ethical fantasy begins, eventually its young protagonist will find herself or himself closely involved in some type of significant action, the culmination of which is crucial in some larger issue calling for a confrontation between good and evil. Typical is Andre Norton's *Steel Magic*. Three ordinary children, Sara, Greg, and Eric, find themselves in a strange, magical world and are caught up in a struggle between good and evil.

> The enemy . . . are those powers of darkness who war against all that is good and fair and right. Wizards of the Black, warlocks, werewolves, ghouls, ogres—the enemy has as many names and faces as Avalon itself— many bodies and disguises, some fair, but mainly foul. They are shadows of the darkness, who have long sought to overwhelm Avalon and then win to victory in other worlds, yours among them. Think of what you fear and hate the most, and that will be part of the enemy and the Dark Powers. ("Cold Iron")

Although the children are understandably not too eager to join the fray, Merlin points out to them that the struggle is for real and their involvement is necessary: "Then you can understand why we are excited at your coming. We lose three talismans, and then you arrive.

What else can we believe but that your fate is tied to our loss?" ("Merlin's Mirror")

Furthermore, to be involved effectively, they must take sides, choosing between good and evil, a choice they eventually find the courage to make:

> "Then I choose to do as you wish," Greg answered. "It's for Dad, in a way." He looked questioningly at Sara and Eric.
> "All right." Eric's agreement was reluctant. He looked as scared and unhappy as Sara felt inside.
> She held to the basket which was the only real thing now in this mixed-up dream. And her voice was very small and thin as she said, "Me, I'll help too," though she did not want to at all. ("Merlin's Mirror")

After the victory of the forces of good under King Arthur's leadership, Sara, Greg, and Eric are content to be publicly praised for their important contribution: "Also know this—Avalon gives thanks and Avalon cherishes her own. For you are now a part of her, which in time to come may be more to you than you can now guess." ("The Fox Gate")

The young protagonists of heroic-ethical fantasy must decide to become involved, distinguish good from evil, and see good triumph. If these essential components are presented simplistically, forecast too soon, or made the occasion for preaching, the story's mission will fail; it will likely be resented or, worse, go unread. Hence, the plots have been written to include a variety of obstacles, hesitations, and uncertainties. Heroic-ethical fantasy, therefore, insures interest, suspense, accurate psychological insight, and broad directionality without prescribing clear solutions. Accordingly, the young protagonists occasionally distrust their ability to discriminate between good and evil. Jesse and Rich, for example, in Jay Williams's The Hero from Otherwhere, are momentarily taken aback by their inability to tell the difference.

> "And I've been thinking. . . . I wonder if that phantom we saw was put there by Skrymir? Or if it could have been Skrymir himself."
> "We're going to have an awful time recognizing the enemy, . . . How can we tell who he is? He might be anybody." (chapter 9)

In Garner's The Weirdstone of Brisingamen, for another example, Fenodyree cautions Colin and Susan that the evil foe, the morthbrood, "mingle with others unnoticed, and can be detected only by certain marks, and that not always" (chapter 16). On another occasion Colin, this time in *The Moon of Gomrath*, is confused as he learns that Pelis's being a dwarf does not assure his siding with the cause of goodness. "Why's he doing all this? . . . we didn't think twice about trusting him, with him being a dwarf" (chapter 18).

Another device that adds plausibility and suspense to the plot calls for the young protagonists, facing a potentially dangerous situation that requires their help or participation, to debate their options before a positive decision is made. In *The Hero from Otherwhere*, Jesse and Rich appreciate the significance of their actions and the necessity of acting positively. Rich says,

" . . . and when he said that about saving our world and this one I felt that if I didn't speak up, I'd never be able to look myself in the face again." Jesse agrees:

> "But I felt I was making the choice he'd have made if he had been in my place. It made me feel good."
> "Yeah. That's right." (chapter 8)

Very clearly and perhaps even too directly Mary Stewart in *A Walk in Wolf Wood* depicts her protagonists, John and Margaret, pondering their options.

> I do not think that John and Margaret were any braver or better than most children. Besides, in spite of what Mardian had said, they tended still to think that such a strange experience could only be a dream, and so there could be no real danger to them, whatever they undertook to do. It was a storybook adventure, no more, and they would waken from it the moment danger threatened, to find themselves safely back in their own familiar world. And, like any other children who read a lot of stories, they believed that this one must end happily, . . . They knew that if you find some person or creature in desperate need or help which you can supply, you have a human duty to supply it, even if it could inconvenience or even hurt you to do so. This . . . is how the greatest and best deeds in the world have been done, and though the children did not say this aloud, they knew it inside themselves without even thinking about it. (chapter 7)

A more dramatic and hence more poignant instance of the emotional intensity attending making ethical choices occurs in Victor Kelleher's *Master of the Grove*, when Derin is challenged to decide between his liberty or the life of Marna, to whom he is obligated but about whom he feels most ambivalent.

> "It was bad enough following at your heels," he said angrily to Marna. "Must I now be at Krob's beck and call?"
>
> "You are the one who wanted to be free," Marna reminded him. "Didn't you realize that all we can ever hope for is the freedom to choose? And that you have always had. So come, boy, make your decision." Her voice was even and steady, betraying no sign of fear.
>
> "Don't you even care about your own life?" he said, exasperated by her. "Are you too proud to plead?"
>
> "The time for pleading is past," she answered. . . .
>
> With a muttered curse, Derin turned towards the mountains.
>
> "Spare her," he said bitterly. "I accept your bargain; her life for my freedom." (chapter 12)

So common has this device become that L'Engle employs an interesting variant in *A Swiftly Tilting Planet* when young Charles, already eager to make the right decision but momentarily stymied as to what exactly he should do, is tempted by the false unicorn to act too soon.

> [Y]ou have the ability to see the difference between right and wrong, and to make the correct decisions. You were selected because you are an extraordinary young man and your gifts and your brains qualify you. You are the only one who can control the Might-Have-Been. . . . Come, Charles Wallace. You have been chosen. You are in control of what is going to happen. You are needed. We must go. (chapter 10)

Still another device that adds plausibility and suspense involves an apparently inconsequential action that has results of great importance. Taran neglects to provide for Hen Wen's security. During a raid, the magic pig runs away in fear; the boy impulsively takes after it and stumbles upon the Horned King. The resulting series of adventures—Alexander's Prydain chronicles—culminate in Taran's becoming High King. Robert and Jennifer of Margaret Anderson's *In the Circle of Time*, who are interested in old legends, dig haphazardly among some old stones near their home and trigger their passage into the future where they assist in defeating the Barbaric Ones who threaten civilization. Resenting the older Jasper's rank, young Ged in Le Guin's *A Wizard of Earthsea* seeks to prove the superiority of his magic by summoning back the dead; doing so successfully, he also calls up an evil shadow that dogs his steps. When the boy makes up his mind to stop fleeing the shadow and, instead, face it openly, he unknowingly takes the one essential step toward ultimately learning his true nature. Paul Fisher's *The Hawks of Fellheath* provide another example. When one of his friends unexpectedly sets out to locate what he believes is the Emperor's country, where the dead live again, Mole sets out after him, only to get caught up in the war with the wicked King Ichodred and his evil wizard, the Black Counselor, with whom Mole dramatically is called upon to engage in a hand-to-hand combat to death. L'Engle's *A Wrinkle in Time* contains an especially apt instance of this third device. Overconfident in his genius, Charles Wallace believes he can successfully challenge the malevolent "It" but is defeated and imprisoned with his father. His sister, Meg, on the other hand, convinced that she is the only member of the Murry family who possesses no distinctive gift or capacity, is greatly surprised when her fervent, unconditional declaration of love for her father and brother not only frees them but even repulses the Evil threatening the entire world. Besides adding suspense and complexity, the device of the unexpected or unintended result has one other advantage. It graphically suggests to young readers that their actions and choices, whether small or large, matter in their lives and in the lives of others and sometimes may even have widespread consequences.

One final reason why heroic-ethical fantasy actively invites young readers' positive responses and empathic identifications is its ability to depict both traditional heroism and the kind of heroism most young people are likely to be called upon to manifest. For every Peter and Edmund Pevensie (*The Lion, the Witch, and the Wardrobe*), John (*The Beginning Place*), or Walter the Earl (*The Gammage Cup*) who takes sword in hand and actually performs conventional heroic deeds—such as slaying evil creatures, dragons, or Mushrooms—there are far more protagonists whose deeds are less dramatic and overtly heroic but paradoxically prove just as decisive in vanquishing evil. Before Curley Green, Walter the Earl, Muggies, Gummy, and Mingy actually have to fight the Mushrooms with sword and arrow in Kendall's *The Gammage Cup*, they have to overcome first their own timidity and then the repressive rule of their neighbors who order the five's banishment. In *The Tombs of Atuan*, Le Guin does not depict young Ged, who is already on the way to becoming the greatest Mage in Earthsea's history, as executing some stupendously heroic task. Rather, Le Guin has him complete the far more prosaic task of saving the priestess Arha from her passivity and the devouring Dark Ones, a task he accomplishes by gentleness and courtesy. Fiona and Bran McCool in Tannen's *The Wizard Children of Finn* contribute to Finn's ultimate victory by becoming bards: Fiona composes the verse that will recount for posterity the hero Finn's various adventures, while her younger brother memorizes his sister's verse so that it can be recited later to prove Finn's heroic stature. And in Bellairs's *The House with a Clock in Its Walls*, Lewis foils the plan of the wicked Izzard witches to hasten the Day of Judgment, when the Lord and Master of Black Evil will come, by seizing a ticking clock and smashing it to the ground. The conflict between a desire to embark upon heroic adventures and the call to do one's duty that may or may not lead to adventure is humorously illustrated in Paul Fisher's *The Ash Staff*, when Mole's talking sword urges him to "hit" the adventure-road.

> "Well," demanded the Sword impatiently. "Are we going or not?"
>
> "Not!" Mole snapped, angry at his own weakness. "I made a promise to Arien and the others—"
>
> "Promises, promises," the Sword sneered, "If I kept all the promises I made, I would still be a bit of iron, no more. My dear boy, people don't become heroes by tending children and keeping pledges. People become heroes by being adventurous, taking chances, and forgetting about dull things like oaths!"
>
> The Sword's use of the word *heroes* made Mole feel quite uncomfortable, but he remained staunchly silent. (chapter 5)

Another author who uses a variety of devices to illustrate and depict both traditional heroism and the kind of heroism most young people will be expected to manifest is Madeleine L'Engle. Perhaps best known for continuing the impact of the Nesbit Legacy through her own work, L'Engle has more than forty works that have contributed to the popularity of both fantasy and science fiction. Like Nesbit, L'Engle combines fantasy and realism, adding a strong element of science fiction to the mix. It is this blend of fantasy and science fiction, perhaps, that causes the difficulty in classifying her work. However, it is precisely this combination that makes for a rich blend and provides the fantasy with a strong rationale. Her fantasy and science fiction so easily mingle with reality that the reader seldom has any trouble synthesizing them throughout the read.

A *Wrinkle in Time*, the first in the series about the Murry family, perhaps best exemplifies L'Engle's skillful melding of fantasy and science fiction. Awarded the Newbery Medal of Honor more than three decades ago and still considered by some to be Madeleine L'Engle's finest novel, A *Wrinkle in Time* is, first of all, a realistic family novel. The Murrys are a close-knit, affectionate, supportive, and intelligent family; these qualities, instead of seeming incredible or tiresomely banal, are both plausible and attractive because they derive from the family's behavior and words. The Murrys' goodness, in particular, is not innate or miraculously accounted for, but earned through hard choice and sacrifice.

Written for preadolescents, this novel honestly portrays its protagonists, Meg Murry and Calvin O'Keefe, in situations typical of many young people—anxiety over physical appearance, unsettled parental relationships, peer and sibling rivalries, and the search for identity. The characterization and prominence of Meg, incidentally, are happy anticipations of the non-sexist female protagonist of today.

Because A *Wrinkle in Time* features a futuristic mode of space travel and speculates about possible life elsewhere in the universe, it can be considered science fiction. As such, it is a historically important book, since it is the first young-adult science fiction novel to be not only admitted into the mainstream of children's literature but also honored in a significant way. It marks the coming of age of science fiction fantasy literature for children and young adults, while incorporating many of the traditional aspects of heroic ethical fantasy.

In order to rescue their father, who has been trapped in another dimension as a result of his scientific experiments with time travel, the protagonists travel to other worlds by means of a "tesseract," a virtual wrinkle in time. As time travel, this could also be considered fantasy as the characters "time slip" between worlds with the aid of three superhuman characters. The novel begins with the line, "It was a dark and stormy night," and the readers are soon introduced to Mrs. Whatsit, Mrs. Which, and Mrs. Who. Whether viewed as three fairy godmothers, witches, or guardian angels, they are described as benevolent, humorous, and most unusual. Mrs. Whatsit first presents herself as what Meg can only describe as a tramp. "It seemed small for Meg's idea of a tramp. The age or sex was impossible to tell, for it was completely bundled up in clothes. Several scarves of assorted colors were tied about the head, and a man's felt hat was perched atop. A shocking pink stole was knotted about a rough overcoat, and black rubber boots covered the feet" (22). "Mrs. Whatsit untied a blue and green paisley scarf, a red and yellow flowered print, a gold Liberty print, a red and black bandanna. Under all this a sparse quantity of grayish hair was tied in a small but tidy knot on top of her head. Her eyes were bright, her nose a round, soft blob, her mouth puckered like an autumn apple" (23). These lovable beings have the ability to transmorph, verbalize, and fly through time and space. Later, Meg and Charles Wallace, and Calvin ride through space and time on Mrs. Whatsit's back.

> Her plump little body began to shimmer, to quiver, whitened. The pudding-bag shape stretched, lengthened, merged. And suddenly before the children was a creature more beautiful than Meg had ever imagined, and the beauty lay in far more than the outward description. Outwardly, Mrs. Whatsit was surely no longer a Mrs. Whatsit. She was a marble white body with powerful flanks, something like a horse but at the same time completely unlike a horse, for from the magnificently modeled back sprang a nobly formed torso, arms, and a head resembling a man's, but a man with a perfection of dignity and virtue, and exaltation of joy such as Meg had never seen before . . . From the shoulders slowly a pair of wings unfolded, wings made of rainbows, of light upon water, of poetry. (63)

Additional gothic elements and multiple references to Shakespeare's *Macbeth* strengthen the fantasy. The magic spectacles of Mrs. Who allow Meg to pass through walls. Later, when Meg's body has been taxed to its limit by tessering, the gentle Aunt Beast nurses her back to health. And finally, at the end of the novel, Mrs. Whatsit, Mrs.

Who, and Mrs. Which, their task completed, disappear in a gust of wind.

Beyond the elements of mixed fantasy, L'Engle includes those of the heroic-ethical tradition. *Wrinkle in Time* is ultimately concerned with the theme of good versus evil and through the protagonists' adventures, they gradually come of age in their ability to discern right from wrong. The plot and theme support the consistent order of the universe and stress that there is always order, even when as humans we cannot determine why. In a discussion with her mother, Meg asks if things always have an explanation. Her mother answers, "Yes, I believe that they do. But I think that with our human limitations we're not always able to understand the explanations. But you see, Meg, just because we don't understand doesn't mean that the explanation doesn't exist" (47). Further themes of fallibility and patience are woven throughout this novel, and the young protagonists learn that they must act together when the father is unable to solve everything himself.

Second in the series is *A Wind in the Door*, the title taken from Malory's *Le Morte d'Arthur*. L'Engle increases the elements of mixed fantasy and heroic-ethical tradition in this novel, and on page one, young Charles Wallace announces the appearance of dragons in the vegetable garden. Charles Wallace is ill, and human medicine is unable to help. His mother, who has two Ph.D.s in science and just happens to be researching mitochondria, is unable to help him, and the children are once again challenged to work together in order to save him.

As science fiction, there is much discussion of biology, in particular the function of mitochondria and farandolae, as the young protagonists, Meg and Calvin, and their school principal, Mr. Jenkins, enter into the bloodstream of Charles Wallace to fight the forces of evil in order to heal him. As with *A Wrinkle in Time*, they are assisted in this scientific adventure by a friendly dragon who is really not a dragon at all.

> Yes. Charles Wallace's drive of dragons was a single creature, although Meg was not at all surprised that Charles Wallace had confused this fierce, wild being with dragons. She had the feeling that she never saw all of it at once, and which of all the eyes could she meet? Merry eyes, wise eyes, ferocious eyes, kitten eyes, dragon eyes, opening and closing, looking at her, looking at Charles Wallace and Calvin and the strange tall

man. And wings, wings in constant motion, covering and uncovering the eyes. When the wings were spread out they had a span of at least ten feet, and when they were all folded in, the creature resembled a misty, feathery sphere. Little spurts of flame and smoke spouted up between the wings: it could certainly start a grass fire if it weren't careful. (56)

The strange, tall man identifies himself as "A Teacher" and introduces the children to Proginoskes, a cherub with a sense of humor. Blageny, the teacher of both Proginoskes and the children, explains that it must be Meg and Calvin who help Charles Wallace. In order to do so they must pass three tests or trials that they must not only complete but first discover what they are. Meg discovers that her first task is to be a "namer," bestowing identity to earthlings in order to make them feel more human. As Proginoskes tells her, "If your name isn't known, then it's a very lonely feeling" (79).

Further elements of mixed fantasy are inextricably intertwined with science. A childhood pet, Louise the Larger, is a harmless black garden snake named after longtime family friend and physician, Dr. Louise Colubra. The snake plays a role in the protection of the children and transforms into a hissing cobra, coiled and ready to strike, and succeeds in scaring off the evil force who has assumed the appearance of Mr. Jenkins. "Mr. Jenkins screamed, in a way that she had never known a man could scream a high, piercing screech. Then he rose up into the night like a great, flapping bird, flew, screaming across the sky, became a rent, an emptiness, a slash of nothingness—" (49). The evil one is actually the Echthroi, those who hate and unname. Later, we find out that Louise the Larger is actually a colleague of Blageny.

The second test is to save Charles Wallace, and the third is to save the real Mr. Jenkins. Again in this work, L'Engle stresses the themes of good versus evil and the interconnectedness of all things. In discovering that they are all part of one another, Meg, Calvin, and Mr. Jenkins literally become a minute part of Charles Wallace as they travel into his bloodstream. In successfully completing their quests, the protagonists recognize the power and importance of every living thing. "It is a pattern throughout creation. One child, one man, can swing the balance of the universe" (173).

Third in the series of the Murry family is A *Swiftly Tilting Planet*. Set at the time of the Thanksgiving holiday, the unseasonable weather foreshadows the events to come. "There's something wrong with the weather. There's something wrong," warns Meg (9). Recently married to Meg, Calvin O'Keefe is with his mother at the Murrys' for holiday dinner, and Mrs. O'Keefe chants an ancient Irish rune to ward off danger. When she repeats the chant, this time with Charles Wallace, the weather calms down. She later tells Charles Wallace, "You've got it, Chuck. Use it" (23). Kything or communicating without speech is used again in this novel and is apparently used as well by the Murrys' new stray dog. As Meg and the dog kythe the whereabouts of Charles Wallace, who has gone outside to the visit the favorite stargazing rock, we view him again calling on the heavens, this time for direction. A beam of light shoots down from a single star beside Charles Wallace, and "slowly the radiance took on form, until it had enfleshed itself into the body of a great, white beast with flowing main and tail. From its forehead sprang a silver horn that contained the residue of light. It was a creature of absolute perfection" (44). This unicorn, Gaudior, doesn't actually speak but kythes or telepathically communicates with Charles Wallace and charges him with a quest. Because the various worlds are connected, it is necessary for Charles Wallace to join Gaudior in traveling to fight the Echthroi, the ancient enemy. Charles hops aboard and together they ride the wind into the past and the future in order to find the evil Echthroi.

Through their travels, Charles Wallace actually becomes various characters, from the mediaeval to the Puritan times, each time within the characters involved, successfully completing the quest before him, each time diverting disaster. Charles Wallace continues his travels with Gaudior, following the story of the twins through time. Eventually, he changes history to avert nuclear holocaust. Together, they discover the story of Mrs. O'Keefe (Beezie), and she ultimately saves Charles Wallace by invoking the old Irish rune and putting herself between them and the forces of evil. In reference to combining the themes of fantasy and science fiction, L'Engle has the character Beezie state, "I don't much like science fiction. I like fairy tales better" (181).

The fourth in the Murry family series is *Many Waters*. The twins, Sandy and Dennys, while in their parents' laboratory, interrupt an experiment in progress and after typing "someplace warm and sparsely populated" (9) time-slip into the time of Noah, before the great flood. Here they meet seraphim and nephalim who take the forms of animals—the seraphim as scarab beetles, pelicans, and mammoths, the nephalim as snakes, rats, and vultures. In this book, too, the characters are able to communicate telepathically without speech, referred to in this novel as "underhearing" in the old language before Babel.

The mammoth has the ability to transform into a unicorn, and other mythical beasts are also present, including a manticore, a dragon, and a griffin. Later, Grandfather Lamech rubs the scarab beetle like a magic lamp and a seraph, Adnarel, appears.

> Then came a vivid flash of light, similar to that of a unicorn's horn, and a tall presence stood in the tent, smiling at the old man, then looking quietly at Sandy. The personage had skin the same glowing apricot color as Yalith's. Hair the color of wheat with the sun on it, brightly gold, long, and tied back, falling so that it almost concealed tightly furled wings, the light-filled gold of the hair. The eyes were an incredibly bright blue, like the sea with sunlight touching the waves. (39)

The twins help Noah build the ark and then devise a plan to get home through time and space with the help of the unicorns and the seraphim. Again, this novel combines elements of journey fantasy, transformation, and talking animals with the heroic-ethical themes of good versus evil and coming of age. The twins, who have always been more pragmatic than their sister Meg, have always been doubtful about the existence of magic. Toward the end of the novel, however, they need the help of the unicorns to return home, and since the only way that unicorns will appear is if you believe in them, Sandy and Dennys find it necessary to cast away their doubt. As Sandy is told by the mammoth/unicorn, "Some things have to be believed to be seen" (256).

Fifth in the series of the O'Keefe family, *An Acceptable Time*, finds Polly O'Keefe (daughter of Meg Murry and Calvin O'Keefe) once again adventuring into unknown worlds. This time, Polly drops through a "time gate" into a land of druids and human sacrifice. Again, the star-watching rock plays an important role, acting as Meg's "threshold" through time. Although she remains in the same location, she is transported back three thousand years and meets two druids, Anarel and Karralys who are also able to "slip" into the twentieth century. Anarel explains to Polly that when circles of time overlap, a threshold opens and people are able to cross over into the other time. Karralys believes that Polly has been brought over in order to help them in their time of civil unrest.

The story is set during the week of All Hallows' Eve or Halloween, corresponding with "Samhaim," the Celtic New Year. We learn that the Christian church renamed the pagan holiday "All Saints Day" in the eighth century and that during holy times, the gates between times swing open more easily. Polly also learns that her grandparents' farm is a former holy site, and although warned by her grandparents to stay away, Polly is encouraged by her friend Zachary to cross over. Together they become involved in a war between two druid tribes, one wishing to use Polly as human sacrifice to bring the rains. While Polly tries to mediate the conflict and avoid her own death, her friend Zachary is only intent on getting the medicine people to heal his heart defect. Selfish and careless, Polly is also forced to rescue him before she can return in time and guarantee her own safety.

Whether by magic or metaphysics, the druids heal Zachary's heart, and the large black garden snake, Louise the Larger, travels back in time to help rescue Polly when she calls for help. Polly avoids becoming the human sacrifice, assists in building a new alliance between the two tribes, and Zachary is healed. The only sacrifice that is asked is the sacrifice of love, and "the lines of love cross time and space" (340), reminding us that love is greater than hate.

Within the stories of the Murry family, we have time slips, talking snakes, and guardian angel icons. L'Engle successfully blends fantasy, history, religion, science, and heroic ethical traditions into a workable whole. The reader is warned to temper belief in science with universal truths that may not be scientifically provable. "Truth is eternal. Knowledge is changeable. It is disastrous to confuse them" (91).

Coming of Age

In much of the world today, coming of age, the successful passage from childhood to adulthood, is no longer marked by public rite or celebrated communally, as primitive societies once did and in some places still do. Instead, for many people, adolescence itself serves as a coming of age, and its completion upon reaching a certain chronological age as prescribed by law—being old enough to vote, join the military, enter into legally binding contracts, or drink alcoholic beverages—marks the attainment of adulthood and is usually a private matter involving individuals, their families, and sometimes friends. Still, sociologists and psychologists disagree among themselves exactly when childhood and puberty cease and adulthood begins; yet virtually all concur that to be adult implies a capacity to admit that one is finite, to accept responsibility for one's actions and one's life, and to choose and act autonomously, and to be, in consequence, capable of evil. Regardless of his or her legal status or chronological age, any individual who demonstrates such capacity, then, is rightly considered an adult; that person has come of age. Children's literature is rightfully and seriously concerned with coming of age as subject matter and theme. The young adult novel, so popular today, derives much of its popularity from the fact that it explicitly deals with the issues young people confront during adolescence—physical changes, acne, peer relationships, dating, drugs, alcohol, sex, career anxiety and decisions, relations with parents, loneliness, suicide—and suggests that, by and large, the dilemmas associated with them are manageable and solvable.

Heroic-ethical fantasy in particular can be a very effective dramatization of coming of age. An example that accommodates this theme is the typical scenario of a young protagonist, caught up in a struggle between good and evil, who performs, despite adverse circumstances, some deed that results in a favorable outcome for the good. One of the most well developed and, therefore, satisfying portraits of coming of age in children's heroic-ethical fantasy is that of Taran, the hero of the Prydain chronicles, who belatedly recognizes that to be Assistant Pig-Keeper is not identical to being a "pig boy." Through five books Alexander candidly, with humor and affection, shows Taran's sometimes painful growth from a feckless and naive youth, impatient with irksome responsibilities, eager to action, and lured by dreams of glory, to a seasoned and disciplined man whose sense of duty, unselfishness, and willingness to help others earn him the High Kingship of Prydain. Noteworthy in Alexander's portrait of Taran is his gradual realization that heroism is not given by birth or rank, the passage of time, or magic.

Instead, it must be earned. To strive to be oneself, to do what one must, and to accept human finitude are genuinely heroic. Other examples include Ged's coming of age in Le Guin's *A Wizard of Earthsea*, Arha's in her *The Tombs of Atuan*, and Hugh and Irene's in her *The Beginning Place*, as well as Peter's in *A String in the Harp* (Bond), Mole's in *The Ash Staff* (Fisher), Meg's in L'Engle's *A Wrinkle in Time* and Charles Wallace's in her *A Swiftly Tilting Planet*, and Derin's in *Master of the Grove* (Kelleher).

Perhaps because she has been successful in utilizing heroic-ethical fantasy to portray coming of age in the Earthsea trilogy and *The Beginning Place* and has even written a young adult novel, Ursula Le Guin has argued that fantasy actually may be more effective than realistic fiction in assisting young readers to come to grips imaginatively with adolescence. Maneuvering through that period of life, she suggests, is basically a journey to "self-knowledge, to adulthood, to the light," a journey young people can successfully complete, if they follow as guide the Shadow. Le Guin describes it as "all we don't want to, can't, admit into our conscious self, all the qualities and tendencies within us that have been repressed, denied, or not used ("The Child," 64). Fantasy and not realistic fiction is the "medium best suited to a description of that journey" because "the events of a voyage into the unconscious are not describable in the language of rational daily life: only the symbolic language of the deeper psyche will fit them without trivializing them" (65).

This journey is moral as well as psychological and involves struggle—a pattern similar to the plots of heroic-ethical fantasy.

> Most great fantasies contain a very strong, striking moral dialectic, often expressed as a struggle between the Darkness and the Light. But that makes it sound simple, and the ethics of the unconscious—of the dream, the fantasy, the fairy tale—are not simple at all. They are, indeed, very strange. (65–66)

Le Guin rightly warns against simplistic or mechanical renditions of both the journey and struggle, whether in realism or fantasy. Even heroic-ethical fantasy can be trivialized, its scenario oversimplified or routinely depicted, as happened unfortunately in Robert Newman's *The Shattered Stone*, which, despite containing all the essential parts of the scenario, puts them together with little grace and subtlety. Further, Le Guin believes that realism far too often succumbs to the temptation to reduce the evil of the world, both real and potential, to "problems," the answers to which can be looked up, so to speak, at the back of the book. On the other hand, fantasy is paradoxically more realistic than realism because it tends to view evil as it is, an element in life that is not going away overnight. Evil is irrational and perhaps fundamental (69).

Although Le Guin does not speak explicitly of broad directionality, one might infer that she would be sympathetic to the suggestion that that quality also explains the superiority of fantasy over realism as a medium for rendering coming of age. Broad directionality, as previously stated, refers to the capacity of heroic-ethical fantasy to suggest a variety of options, without threats or judgments to young readers who may be confronted with a particular issue or concern—creative options visualized as result of reading fantasy. On the contrary, realistic fiction can have a limiting effect on problem solving, since the events, circumstances, and settings are so true to life that readers may have difficulty imagining other solutions. Readers may very well reject solutions, even the correct ones, if they see them as forced. Further, if a particular solution that realism proposes is adopted and the "problem" should continue, the reader may experience even greater guilt or anxiety: If it worked for X, why doesn't it work for me? Is it, then, my fault? Heroic-ethical fantasy does not insist but suggests, does not furnish solutions but guides, and does not judge but affirms and supports. Consequently, heroic-ethical fantasy is didactic in the best sense of the word and not moralistic or proselytizing: It teaches, it challenges, and, never to be overlooked, it entertains.

Works Cited and Other Titles Mentioned

Alexander, Lloyd. *The Black Cauldron*. New York: Holt, 1965.
——. *The Book of Three*. New York: Holt, 1964.
——. *The Castle of Llyr*. New York: Holt, 1966.
——. *The First Two Lives of Lukas-Kasha*. New York: Dutton, 1978.
——. *The High King*. New York: Holt, 1968.
——. *Taran Wanderer*. New York: Holt, 1967.
Anderson, Margaret. *In the Circle of Time*. New York: Knopf, 1979.

Bellairs, John. *The House with a Clock in Its Walls*. New York: Dial, 1973.

Bond, Nancy. *A String in the Harp*. New York: Atheneum, 1976.

Cameron, Eleanor. "High Fantasy: A *Wizard of Earthsea*." *Horn Book Magazine*, vol. 47 (December 1971).

Cooper, Susan. *The Dark Is Rising*. New York: Macmillan, 1973.

——. *Greenwitch*. New York: Atheneum, 1974.

——. *Over Sea, Under Stone*. New York: Scholastic, 1965.

Curry, Jane Louise. *The Mysterious Shrinking House*. New York: Scholastic, 1965.

——. *The Sleepers*. New York: Harcourt, 1968.

Fisher, Paul. *The Ash Staff*. New York: Atheneum, 1979.

——. *The Hawks of Fellheath*. New York: Atheneum, 1980.

Frye, Northrup. *The Educated Imagination*. Bloomington, Ind.: Indiana University Press, 1964.

Garner, Alan. *Elidor*. New York: Walck, 1965.

——. *The Moon of Gomrath*. New York: Walck, 1967.

——. *The Weirdstone of Brisingamen*. New York: Walck, 1968.

Harding, D. W. "Psychological Processes in the Reading of Fiction." In *The Cool Web: The Pattern of Children's Reading*, edited by Margaret Meek, Aidan Warlow, and Griselda Barton. New York: Atheneum, 1978.

Jones, Diane Wynne. *Power of Three*. New York: Pantheon, 1965.

Kelleher, Victor. *Master of the Grove*. Harmondsworth, UK: Puffin, 1983.

Kendall, Carol. *The Gammage Cup*. New York: Harcourt, 1959.

Le Guin, Ursula. *The Beginning Place*. New York: Harper, 1980.

——. *The Farthest Shore*. New York: Atheneum, 1972.

——. *The Tombs of Atuan*. New York: Atheneum, 1971.

——. *A Wizard of Earthsea*. New York: Bantam, 1975.

——. "The Child and the Shadow," in *The Language of the Night: Essays in Fantasy and Science Fiction*. New York: Perigee, 1979.

L'Engle, Madeleine. *An Acceptable Time*. New York: Dell, 1989.

——. *Many Waters*. New York: Farrar, Straus & Giroux, 1986.

——. *A Swiftly Tilting Planet*. New York: Farrar, Straus & Giroux, 1980.

——. *A Wind in the Door*. New York: Farrar, Straus & Giroux, 1973.

——. *A Wrinkle in Time*. New York: Farrar, Straus & Giroux, 1962.

Lewis, C. S. *The Last Battle*. New York: Macmillan, 1956.

——. *The Lion, the Witch, and the Wardrobe*. New York: Macmillan, 1951.

——. *The Magician's Nephew*. New York: Macmillan, 1970.

——. *The Voyage of the Dawn Treader*. New York: Macmillan, 1952.

Lively, Penelope. *The Whispering Knights*. New York: Dutton, 1976.

Mayne, Willliam. *Earthfasts*. New York: Dutton, 1967.

Molson, Francis J. "Ethical Fantasy for Children." In *The Aesthetics of Fantasy Literature and Art,* edited by Roger C. Schlobin. South Bend, Ind.: University of Notre Dame Press, 1982.

Nesbit, Edith. *The Enchanted Castle.* New York: Dent, 1968.

Newman, Robert. *The Shattered Stone.* New York: Atheneum, 1975.

Nichols, Ruth. *The Marrow of the World.* New York: Atheneum, 1972.

Norton, Andre. *Steel Magic.* New York: Archway, 1978.

Rowling, J. K. *Harry Potter and the Chamber of Secrets.* New York: Scholastic, 1999.

———. *Harry Potter and the Goblet of Fire.* New York: Scholastic, 2000.

———. *Harry Potter and the Prisoner of Azkaban.* New York: Scholastic, 1999.

———. *Harry Potter and the Sorcerer's Stone.* New York: Scholastic, 1998.

Siegel, Robert. *Alpha Centauri.* Westchester, Ill.: Cornerstone, 1980.

Stewart, Mary. *A Walk in Wolf Wood.* New York: Morrow, 1980.

Tannen, Mary. *The Lost Legend of Finn.* New York: Knopf, 1982.

———. *The Wizard Children of Finn.* New York: Knopf, 1981.

Tolkien, J. R. R. *The Hobbit.* New York: Houghton, 1966.

Tymm, Marshall B., Kenneth J. Zahorski, and Robert H. Boyer. *Fantasy Literature: A Core Collection and Reference Guide.* New York: R. R. Bowker, 1979.

Williams, Jay. *The Hero from Otherwhere.* New York: Walck, 1972.

CHAPTER FIVE

~

Conclusions

The Importance of Fantasy

To experience what has come to be called a good read—enjoying a story that quickly catches a reader's attention, retains it throughout the reading, and all the time entertains—best explains why children over the years have been and continue to be attracted to fantasy. By now, our discussion of the nature and value of fantasy, the various types and subtypes of children's fantasy, the many interesting topics covered, the often provocative themes dramatized, and the relatively high level of artistic achievement found in children's fantasy should have convincingly demonstrated the rich imaginative experience fantasy affords children (and many adults too).

Because this is an experience that cannot be found elsewhere—at least in the same degree of intensity—it would definitely be a shame if young people were not able to enjoy it before leaving childhood. It may be more than a coincidence that many literary historians and critics mark the beginning of genuinely imaginative literature for children— literature that stresses entertainment rather than didacticism—with the publication of Carroll's two Alice narratives, fantasies both delightful and stimulating. The prospect of a "good read," then, is the prime reason for introducing children to fantasy at a very young age.

Unfortunately, there are adults who still do not consider the prospect of a good read sufficient reason for accepting or endorsing the value of fantasy in the lives of children and, therefore, do not recommend it to young people, regardless of what the latter may like or enjoy. Perhaps, influenced by the residual American Puritanism, many adults continue to be uncomfortable with the notion that pleasure can be a prime motive for reading and insist upon a reading fare for children that is overtly moralistic. "What's the moral?" they will ask of a fantasy. "What truth does the story endorse? What in this reading will help my child become a better person?" they will further question. Or, although willing to acknowledge that today's children "deserve," as their elders do, a literature that is both interesting and entertaining to them, these adults may prefer to promote children's fiction that clearly reinforces their own personal values. And fantasy, these adults suspect, advocates or reinforces escapism. In either instance, these adults may not believe that fantasy is well written, serious, and worthwhile. If there is to be any chance of altering their position, these adults need to be informed and reminded of the various rationales that have been proposed for children's fantasy and its subtypes.

Building on the insights of Jean Piaget, F. André Favat has argued that today the fairy tale, despite its roots in and its centuries-long service as adult literature, has special meaning for the very young. Favat's argument is simple and provocative. Most adults, who are understandably preoccupied with living in the real world, forget that this world is not identical to the one that occupies the consciousness of the young. Instead, the child's world surprisingly approximates the world reflected in fairy tales. To be precise, the world as understood by small children shares with the world of fairy tales a belief in the validity of magic. It is a world where the child is central, where participation is important, where animals and toys can have feelings, where evil is punishable, and where actions have consequences.

Favat's contention that the fairy tale is a "natural" literature for children is supported by the findings of Evelyn Pitcher and Ernst Prelinger in their study of young children's story making and telling, *Children Tell Stories: An Analysis of Fantasy*. Their study demonstrates conclusively that fantasy, both as process and result, is natural to young people and as such, fundamental in their lives. Pitcher and Prelinger show that, given the opportunity and without adult prompting and direction, children as young as two years old make up stories, that their stories clearly are fantasy, and that children, regardless of gender or background, are good at making up stories. Unfortunately, this creativity and ability, unless bolstered and reinforced, can diminish, even disappear, by the age of seven or eight. If fostering creativity in children is important, if not essential, they maintain, anything that not only promises to enhance creativity but actually delivers on that promise is useful and desirable—and, because it reawakens or expands the human capacity to perceive and experience wonder, fantasy is effective in stimulating creativity. Exposure to literary fantasy, therefore, should prove useful in either maintaining or revitalizing young people's capacity to make up stories imaginatively. Further, Pitcher and Prelinger find that young people, upon being exposed to television, begin to reflect that medium in their storytelling and, losing originality and freshness, turn conventional and imitative. For the same reason, it can be argued that exposure to literary fantasy may prove effective in negating some of the deleterious influence of television.

The other rationales for fantasy already mentioned—those of Lüthi, Bettelheim, and Le Guin—can be conveniently grouped since they all concentrate on fantasy's important contribution to the normal, healthy maturation of youth. Although he does not use the term explicitly, Lüthi is actually referring to storying—the process whereby the mind fundamentally structures and makes sense out of reality as it impinges upon the individual consciousness—when he speaks of the imagery of "the story-book world." This storybook world, which is derived from listening to or reading fairy tales, enters the "treasure of our imagination" and actively assists in "the building of our world view." Although he also uses the term implicitly, Bettelheim incorporates the process of storying into his defense of fairy tales and, by extension, fantasy. A dislike of his Freudianism or an unhappiness over some of his analyses of individual tales should not obscure Bettelheim's essential point that the fairy tale allows children ample opportunity to expand the repertoire of options and scenarios they must use to impose order upon and make sense of the world they encounter.

In Elizabeth Cook's *The Ordinary and the Fabulous*, a similar reference to the process of storying can be observed in her presentation of the ways myth, legend, and fairy tale can be productively employed by teachers and storytellers. In her explanation of their importance, Cook underscores the point that the Secondary World, found in myth, legend, and fairy tale, is "impressed" with patterns—such as promises kept and broken, testing, wandering and quest, struggle, light and darkness—that a reader can discern in his or her experience of the primary world (2–3). Further, she utilizes a now familiar argument:

> Childhood reading of symbolic and fantastic tales contributes something irreplaceable to any later experience of literature. It is not so much a matter of recognizing the more obscure classical references in *Paradise Lost* as of accepting a whole mode of expression as both natural and serious. (4–5)

Like Lüthi, Le Guin approaches her subject from a humanist perspective. Throughout her defense of the value of fantasy and its almost unique role in helping young people mature, she takes for granted that, whether embodied as realism or fantasy, a literary portrait of coming of age—the passage from childhood to adulthood—is attractive and useful to young readers. The real importance of fantasy, she argues, is that, because it is broadly directional, less threatening and unsettling, and less inclined to treat the turmoil and concerns of adolescence as "mere" problems, fantasy is more effective than realistic fiction in portraying coming of age. Nevertheless, with her views about adolescence as a period of life in which one journeys to self-knowledge and the "light"—a journey that is best expressed symbolically and involves a fundamental moral struggle between Darkness and the Light—Le Guin is also psychologically oriented. Unlike Bettelheim, however, she is no Freudian. Her view that fantasy's superiority over realism stems from its fondness for symbol and indirection is close to Jungian notions about the role of the Shadow and other archetypes in the unconscious.

Admittedly Jungian in developing her defense of children's fantasy is Ravenna Helson. From the results of experiments that involved adults reading children's fantasy written in the first half of the twentieth century and writing down their responses and interpretations, she claims that the making of fantasy allows its adult writers to reflect and, more importantly, work out certain key stages in the Jungian process of individuation that culminates in the mature acceptance of old age and death (121–34). As the writers rework their childhood, becoming aware of archetypal relationships and developing presumably less ego-centric selves, children reading the resulting fantasies can find "context and expression" for their own feelings and emotional experiences (123). Clearly, then, fantasy is important for both adults and children. Moreover, based on the responses and interpretations of the adult readers in the experiments, Helson suggests that children's fantasy may be divided into six types that reflect stages in the development of adults and may assist children through the periods of stress as well as the opportunities they face as they mature. For instance, in type IV fantasy, written by women, such as Clarke's *The Return of the Twelves*, Kendall's *The Gammage Cup*, and Mary Norton's *The Borrowers*, the stories contain no traditional, legendary material; the protagonists are humorous, clever, and small. The plots are concerned with "finding one's own small place and community" or discovering one's own self-expression; the real antagonist takes form from the various cultural restrictions placed upon the individual seeking his or her true place, and what often happens is an instance of the "big and powerful versus the weak and small" pattern. The subject matter and themes of these stories should appeal to any child being forced to conform to the social mores of grown-ups or beginning his or her struggle for independence. As for the woman writing the fantasy, the theme, Helson indicates, reflects her struggle for self-expression against the power and values of a patriarchal social system (129).

Consistent with the arguments of these theorists, authors such as J. K. Rowling, Philip Pullman, and Diane Duane are engaging young readers in the fantasy genre. The overwhelming popularity of the *Harry Potter* series has created a resurgence of interest in the fantastic, and many readers are rediscovering the works of other contemporary and historical authors of fantasy. Whether it is Harry, Hermione, and Ron, or Lyra and Will Parry, or Nita and Kit, the actions of these young protagonists parallel those of their classical peers. Their adventures are no less provocative than those of Alice, Meg, or Merlyn and certainly offer no more of an imaginative threat. In fact, these characters and the challenges they face clearly delineate the forces of good and evil and the importance in making the right choices. Despite the importance of the social issues embedded within a story or series, or the controversy that surrounds fantasy in general, it is essential to understand that engaging the imagination is a creative process worth nurturing.

A strong case for the importance of fantasy in the lives of children, therefore, can be made. Whether it will persuade every adult uncomfortable with fantasy is highly unlikely, since some people, despite being informed of various rationales for the value of fantasy and its important function in the maturation of young people, will persist in feeling that fantasy is still escapist and, therefore, untrustworthy. For most people, however, the single most persuasive argument in favor of children's fantasy remains the actual reading of the best or representative children's fantasy. The resulting good read is convincing evidence that children's fantasy provides a distinctive imaginative experience—one too good for young people to miss.

Works Cited and Other Titles Mentioned

Bettelheim, Bruno. *The Uses of Enchantment: The Meaning and Importance of Fairytales.* New York: Random House, 1976.

Clarke, Pauline. *The Return of the Twelves.* New York: Morrow, 1965.

Cook, Elizabeth. *The Ordinary and the Fabulous.* Cambridge: Cambridge University Press, 1969.

Duane, Diane. *Deep Wizardry.* New York: Delacorte, 1985.

———. *High Wizardry.* New York: Magic Carpet, 2001.

———. *So You Want to Be a Wizard?* New York: Yearling (reprint), 1992.

———. *A Wizard Abroad.* New York: Magic Carpet, 2001.

———. *Wizard Alone.* New York: Magic Carpet, 2002.

———. *Wizard's Dilemma.* New York: Magic Carpet, 2002.

Favat, F. André. *Child and Tale: The Origins of Interest.* Urbana, Ill.: NCTE, 1977.

Helson, Ravenna. "Fantasy and Self-Discovery." *Horn Book Magazine,* vol. 46, 1970, 121–34.

Kendall, Carol. *The Gammage Cup.* New York: Harcourt, 1959.

Le Guin, Ursula. "The Child and the Shadow," in *The Language of the Night: Essays in Fantasy and Science Fiction.* New York: Perigee, 1979.

Lüthi, Max. *Once Upon a Time: On the Nature of Fairy Tales.* New York: Ungar, 1970.

Norton, Mary. *The Borrowers.* New York: Harcourt, 1953.

Pitcher, Evelyn, and Ernst Prelinger. *Children Tell Stories: An Analysis of Fantasy*. New York: International Universities Press, 1963.

Pullman, Philip. *The Amber Spyglass*. New York: Knopf, 2000.

———. *The Golden Compass*. New York: Knopf, 1996.

———. *The Subtle Knife*. New York: Knopf, 1997.

Rowling, J. K. *Harry Potter and the Chamber of Secrets*. New York: Scholastic, 1999.

———. *Harry Potter and the Goblet of Fire*. New York: Scholastic, 2000.

———. *Harry Potter and the Prisoner of Azkaban*. New York: Scholastic, 1999.

———. *Harry Potter and the Sorcerer's Stone*. New York: Scholastic, 1998.

Bibliography

Aardema, Verna. *Bimiwili and the Zimwi*. Illus. Susan Meddaugh. New York: Dial, 1985.

———. *Who's in Rabbit's House?* Illus. Leo and Diane Dillon. New York: Dial, 1977.

———. *Why Mosquitoes Buzz in People's Ears*. Illus. Leo and Diane Dillon. New York: Dial, 1975.

Adams, Richard. *Watership Down*. New York: Macmillan, 1974.

Adler, C. S. *Good-bye Pink Pig*. New York: Avon, 1985.

Alexander, Lloyd. *The Book of Three*. New York: Holt, 1964.

———. *The Black Cauldron*. New York: Holt, 1965.

———. *The Castle of Llyr*. New York: Holt, 1968.

———. *The First Two Lives of Lukas-Kasha*. New York: Dutton, 1978.

———. *The High King*. New York: Holt, 1968.

———. *The Remarkable Journey of Prince Jen*. New York: Dutton, 1991.

———. *Taran Wanderer*. New York: Holt, 1967.

———. *Time Cat*. New York: Puffin, 1963.

Aliki. *The Story of Johnny Appleseed*. New York: Trumpet, 1963.

Amoss, Bertha. *Lost Magic*. New York: Hyperion, 1993.

Andersen, Hans Christian. "Great Claus and Little Claus," "The Little Match Girl," "The Red Shoes," "The Steadfast Tin Soldier," "The Tinder Box," and "The Ugly Duckling." In *Fairy Tales*. New York: Grosset & Dunlap, 1945.

Anderson, Margaret. *In the Circle of Time*. New York: Knopf, 1979.

Apy, Deborah. *Beauty and the Beast*. Illus. Michael Hague. New York: Holt, Rinehart & Winston, 1980.

Avi. *Bright Shadow*. New York: Macmillan, 1985.

——. *Devil's Race*. New York: Harper Collins, 1984.

——. *The Man Who Was Poe*. New York: Avon, 1989.

——. *Perloo the Bold*. New York: Scholastic, 1998.

——. *Poppy*. Illus. Brian Floca. New York: Avon, 1995.

——. *Poppy and Rye*. Illus. Brian Floca. New York: Avon, 1998.

——. *Something Upstairs*. New York: Avon, 1988.

Babbitt, Natalie. *Tuck Everlasting*. New York: Farrar, 1975.

Bailey, Carolyn. *Miss Hickory*. New York: Viking, 1946.

Banks, Lynne Reid. *The Farthest Away Mountain*. New York: Avon, 1976.

——. *The Indian in the Cupboard*. New York: Doubleday, 1982.

——. *The Mystery of the Cupboard*. New York: Morrow, 1993.

——. *Return of the Indian*. New York: Bantam/Doubleday, 1986.

——. *The Secret of the Indian*. New York: Bantam/Doubleday, 1989.

Barrie, James Matthew. *Peter Pan*. 1911. New York: Bantam, 1985.

Bauer, Marion. *A Taste of Smoke*. New York: Clarion, 1993.

Baum, I. Frank. *The Wonderful Wizard of Oz*. Chicago: Reilly & Lee, 1956.

"BB" [pseud. of D. J. Watkins-Pitchford]. *The Little Grey Men*. New York: Scribner, 1949.

Beatty, Jerome, Jr. *The Tunnel to Yesterday*. New York: Avon, 1983.

Bellairs, John. *The Chessman of Doom*. New York: Dial, 1989.

——. *The Curse of the Blue Figurine*. New York: Dial, 1983.

——. *The Drum, the Doll, and the Zombie*. New York: Dial, 1994.

——. *The Figure in the Shadows*. New York: Dial, 1975.

——. *The Ghost in the Mirror*. New York: Dial, 1993.

——. *The House with a Clock in Its Walls*. New York: Dial, 1973.

——. *The Letter, the Witch, and the Ring*. New York: Dial, 1976.

——. *The Mansion in the Mist*. New York: Puffin, 1992.

——. *The Mummy, the Will, and the Crypt*. New York: Dial, 1983.

——. *The Secret of the Underground Room*. New York: Dial, 1990.

——. *The Spell of the Sorcerer's Skull*. New York: Dial, 1984.

——. *The Trolley to Yesterday*. New York: Dial, 1989.

Berton, Pierre. *The Secret World of Og*. Boston: Little, Brown, 1962.

Block, Francesca Lia. *Weetzie Bat*. New York: Harper Trophy, 1999.

Blount, Margaret. *Animal Land: The Creatures of Children's Fiction*. New York: Avon, 1977.

Bond, Michael. *A Bear Called Paddington*. New York: Houghton, 1960.

Bond, Nancy. *A String in the Harp*. New York: Atheneum, 1976.

Boston, Lucy. *The Children of Green Knowe*. New York: Harcourt, 1967.

———. *The River at Green Knowe*. New York: Harcourt, 1959.

Brett, Jan. *Beauty and the Beast*. New York: Clarion, 1989.

Briggs, Raymond. *The Snowman*. New York: Random House, 1978.

Brooks, Walter R. *Freddy and the Baseball Team from Mars*. New York: Knopf, 1955.

Brown, Marcia. *Once a Mouse. . . .* New York: Macmillan, 1961.

———. *Shadow*. New York: Macmillan, 1982.

Bruchac, Joseph, and Jonathon London. *Thirteen Moons on Turtle's Back*. Illus. Thoms Locker. New York: Philomel, 1992.

Burman, Ben Lucien. *Seven Stars for Catfish Bend*. New York: Avon, 1977.

Burnett, Francis Hodgson. *The Spring Cleaning*. New York: Century, 1908.

———. *The Troubles of Queen Silver-Bell*. New York: Century, 1906.

Carroll, Lewis [Charles Dodgson]. *Alice's Adventures Underground*. 1865.

Carpenter, Humphrey. *The Captain Hook Affair*. Harmondsworth, UK: Puffin, 1982.

Cassedy, Sylvia. *Beyond the Attic Wall*. New York: Avon, 1983.

Christopher, John. *The Guardians*. New York: Macmillan, 1970.

———. *The Prince in Waiting*. New York: Collier, 1970.

———. *The Sword of the Spirits*. New York: Collier, 1972.

Clapp, Patricia. *Jane-Emily*. New York: Lothrop, Lee, 1969.

Clarke, Pauline. *The Return of the Twelves*. New York: Morrow, 1965.

Cleary, Beverly. *The Mouse and the Motorcycle*. New York: Morrow, 1965.

———. *Ralph S. Mouse*. New York: Morrow, 1982.

———. *Runaway Ralph*. New York: Morrow, 1970.

Climo, Shirley. *The Egyptian Cinderella*. Illus. Ruth Heller. New York: Harper, 1989.

Coady, Christopher. *Red Riding Hood*. New York: Dutton, 1991.

Coco, Eugene Bradley. *The Fiddler's Son*. Illus. R. Sabuda. San Diego, Calif.: Green Tiger Press, 1988.

Cole, Judith. *The Moon, the Sun, and the Coyote*. Illus. Cecile Schoberle. New York: Simon & Schuster Books, 1991.

Collodi, Carlo. *Pinocchio*. New York: Macmillan, 1969.

Compton, Patricia. *The Terrible EEK*. Illus. S. Hamanaka. New York: Simon & Schuster, 1991.

Conrad, Pam. *Stonewords: A Ghost Story*. New York: HarperCollins, 1990.

———. *Zoe Rising*. New York: HarperCollins, 1996.

Coombs, Patricia. *Lisa and the Grompet*. New York: Dell, 1980.

Cooney, Caroline B. *Both Sides of Time*. New York: Bantam, 1995.

Cooper, Susan. *The Boggart*. New York: Macmillan, 1993.

———. *The Dark Is Rising.* New York: Macmillan, 1973.

———. *Greenwitch.* New York: Atheneum, 1974.

———. *Over Sea, Under Stone.* New York: Scholastic, 1965.

———. *Seaward.* New York: Atheneum. 1983.

———. *Silver on the Tree.* New York: Atheneum, 1977.

Cox, Marian Roalfe (Andrew Lang, ed.). *Cinderella: Three Hundred and Forty-Five Variants of Cinderella, Catskin, and Cap O'Rushes, Abstracted and Tabulated, with a Discussion of Medieval Analogues and Notes.* London: Folk-Lore Society, 1891. Kraus reprint.

Cross, John Kier [pseud. of Stephen MacFarlane]. *The Other Side of Green Hills.* New York: Coward, 1947.

Curry, Jane Louise. *The Mysterious Shrinking House.* New York: Scholastic, 1965.

———. *The Sleepers.* New York: Harcourt, 1968.

Dahl, Roald. *James and the Giant Peach.* New York: Knopf, 1961.

———. *The Magic Finger.* New York: Harper, 1966.

Dann, Colin. *The Animals of Farthing Wood.* London: Pan, 1980.

Davidson, Lionel. *Under Plum Lake.* New York: Knopf, 1980.

De Brunhoff, Jean. *Babar the Elephant.* New York: Random House, 1937.

De La Mare, Walter. *The Three Mulla-Mulgars.* New York: Knopf, 1919.

Demi. *The Empty Pot.* New York: Trumpet, 1990.

———. *The Magic Boat.* New York: Holt, 1990.

DePaola, Tomi. *Fin M'Coul, The Giant of Knockmany Hill.* New York: Trumpet, 1992.

———. *Strega Nona.* New York: Simon & Schuster, 1975.

De Saint-Exupéry, Antoine. *A Gift of Magic.* New York: Pocket Books, 1971.

———. *The Little Prince.* New York: Harcourt, 1943.

———. *Locked in Time.* New York: Little, Brown, 1976.

———. *The Third Eye.* New York: Little, Brown, 1984.

Duane, Diane. *Deep Wizardry.* New York: Delacorte, 1985.

———. *High Wizardry.* New York: Magic Carpet, 2001.

———. *So You Want To Be a Wizard?* New York: Yearling (reprint) 1992.

———. *A Wizard Abroad.* New York: Magic Carpet, 2001.

———. *Wizard Alone.* New York: Magic Carpet, 2002.

———. *Wizard's Dilemma.* New York: Magic Carpet, 2002.

Duncan, Lois. *Stranger with My Face.* New York: Little, Brown, 1981.

———. *Summer of Fear.* New York: Little, Brown, 1976.

Eager, Edward. *Half Magic.* New York: Harcourt, 1954.

———. *Seven Day Magic.* New York: Harcourt, 1962.

Easton, Samantha. *Beauty and the Beast.* Illus. Ruth Sanderson. Kansas City, Mo.: Andrews McMeel, 1992.

Esbensen, Barbara Juster. *The Star Maiden*. Illus. Helen Davie. New York: Little Brown, 1988.

Farmer, Penelope. *A Castle of Bone*. New York: Atheneum, 1972.

———. *The Summer Birds*. New York: Harcourt, 1962.

Field, Rachel. *Hitty: Her First Hundred Years*. New York: Macmillan 1937.

Fisher, Paul. *The Ash Staff*. New York: Atheneum, 1979.

———. *The Hawks of Fellheath*. New York: Atheneum, 1980.

Fisk, Pauline. *Midnight Blue*. Batavia, Ill.: Lion, 1990.

Fleming, Ian. *Chitty-Chitty Bang Bang*. New York: Random House, 1964.

Forester, C. S. *Poo Poo and the Dragons*. Boston: Little, Brown, 1942.

Furlong, Monica. *Juniper*. New York: Knopf, 1991.

———. *Wise Child*. New York: Knopf, 1987.

Gannett, Ruth Stiles. *My Father's Dragon*. New York: Random House, 1948.

Garner, Alan. *Elidor*. New York: Walck, 1965.

———. *The Moon of Gomrath*. New York: Walck, 1967.

———. *Red Shift*. New York: Macmillan, 1973.

———. *The Weirdstone of Brisingamen*. New York: Walck, 1968.

George, Jean Craighead. *Julie of the Wolves*. New York: Harper & Row, 1972.

Gerstein, Mordecai. *The Mountains of Tibet*. New York: Trumpet, 1987.

Ginsburg, Mirra. *The Chinese Mirror*. Illus. Margot Zemach. New York: Harcourt Brace Jovanovich, 1988.

Gobel, Paul. *Buffalo Woman*. New York: Macmillan, 1984.

———. *The Gift of the Sacred Dog*. New York: Bradbury Press, 1979.

———. *The Great Race of the Birds and Animals*. New York: Macmillan, 1985.

———. *Iktomi and the Boulder*. New York: Orchard, 1988.

———. *Star Boy*. New York: Macmillan, 1983.

Goode, Diane. *Cinderella*. New York: Knopf, 1988.

Gordon, John. *The House on the Brink*. New York: Harper, 1971.

Goudge, Elizabeth. *The Little White Horse*. New York: Coward, 1946.

Gurney, James. *Dinotopia: A Land Apart from Time*. New York, 1992.

Grahame, Kenneth. *The Reluctant Dragon*. New York: Holiday, 1953.

———. *The Wind in the Willows*. New York: Scribner, 1933.

Grimm, Jacob, and Wilhelm Grimm. "The Devil's Three Golden Hairs" ("The Giant with the Three Golden Hairs"), "The Goose Girl," "Rapunzel," "The Twelve Dancing Princesses," and "The White Snake." *Grimms' Fairy Tales*. New York: Grosset & Dunlap, 1945.

———. *Hansel and Gretel*. Illus. Adrienne Adams. New York: Scribner, 1975.

———. *Hansel and Gretel*. Illus. Susan Jeffers. New York: Dial Press, 1980.

———. *Hansel and Gretel*. Illus. Lisbeth Zwerger. New York: Scholastic, 1991 (reprint).

———. *Rapunzel*. Illus. Michael Hague. New York: Creative Education, 1984.

———. *Rapunzel*. Illus. Carol Heyer. Nashville, Tenn.: Ideals Children's Books, 1992.

———. *Rapunzel*. Illus. Felix Hoffman. New York: Harcourt Brace, 1961.

Hahn, Mary Downing. *Time for Andrew: A Ghost Story*. New York: Avon, 1994.

———. *Time of the Witch*. New York: Clarion, 1984.

Haley, Gail E. *A Story a Story*. New York: Macmillan, 1970.

Hamilton, Virginia. *Sweet Whispers, Brother Rush*. New York: Philomel, 1982.

Hoban, Russell. *The Mouse and His Child*. New York: Harper, 1967.

Hodges, Margaret. *Saint George and the Dragon*. Illus. Trina Schart Hyman. Boston: Little, Brown, 1984.

Hogrogian, Nonny. *One Fine Day*. New York: Macmillan, 1971.

Hood, Tom. *Petsetilla's Posy*. New York: Garland, 1976.

Hooks, William. *Moss Gown*. Illus. Donald Carrick. New York: Clarion, 1987.

Hoover, H. M. *The Lost Star*. New York: Puffin, 1986.

———. *Return to Earth*. New York: Puffin, 1988.

Hunter, Mollie. *The Three Day Enchantment*. Illus. Marc Simont. New York: Harper & Row, 1985.

Hyman, Trina Schart. *Little Red Riding Hood*. New York: Holiday House, 1983.

Irving, Washington. *The Legend of Sleepy Hollow*. Illus. Arthur Rackham. New York: Derrydale, 1994.

———. *Rip Van Winkle*. Illus. N. C. Wyeth. New York: Derrydale, 1994.

Jacobs, Joseph. *Tattercoats*. Illus. Margot Tomes. New York: Putnam, 1989.

Jaques, Brian. *The Bellmaker*. New York: Philomel, 1995.

———. *Martin the Warrior*. New York: Philomel, 1993.

———. *Mattimemo*. New York: Philomel, 1990.

———. *Mossflower*. New York: Philomel, 1988.

———. *Muriel of Redwall*. New York: Philomel, 1991.

———. *Redwall*. New York: Philomel, 1986.

Jansson, Tove. *Finn Family Moomintroll*. New York: Avon, 1975.

Jarrell, Randall. *The Animal Family*. New York: Pantheon, 1965.

Jeffers, Susan. *Brother Eagle, Sister Sky*. New York: Dial, 1991.

———. *Hansel and Gretel*. New York: Dutton, 1986.

Jones, Diana Wynne. *Castle in the Air*. New York: Greenwillow, 1990.

———. *Howl's Morning Castle*. New York: Greenwillow, 1987.

———. *Power of Three*. New York: Pantheon, 1965.

Juster, Norton. *The Phantom Tollbooth*. New York: Random House, 1961.

Kafka, Franz. *The Metamorphosis* (1915). Trans. Willa and Edwin Muir. New York: Schocken Books, 1948.

Karlin, Barbara. *Cinderella*. Illus. James Marshall. New York: Trumpet, 1989.

Kelleher, Victor. *Master of the Grove*. Harmondsworth, UK: Puffin, 1983.

Kendall, Carol. *The Gammage Cup*. New York: Harcourt, 1959.

King, Stephen. *Carrie*. New York: Doubleday, 1974.

Kingsley, Charles. *The Water-Babies*. New York: Doubleday, 1954.

Kipling, Rudyard. *The Jungle Books*. New York: Dell, 1964.

Klause, Annette Curtis. *Blood and Chocolate*. New York: Delacorte, 1997.

———. *The Silver Kiss*. New York: Delacorte, 1990.

Kooiker, Leonie. *The Magic Stone*. New York: Morrow, 1978.

Langton, Jane. *The Astonishing Stereoscope*. New York: Harper, 1971.

———. *The Diamond in the Window*. New York: Harper, 1962.

———. *The Fledgling*. New York: Harper, 1980.

———. *The Swing in the Summerhouse*. New York: Harper, 1967.

Lawson, Robert. *Rabbit Hill*. New York: Viking, 1944.

Lee, Jeanne M. *Toad Is the Uncle of Heaven*. New York: Holt, 1985.

Lee, Tanith. *Black Unicorn*. New York: Atheneum, 1991.

Le Guin, Ursula. *The Beginning Place*. New York: Harper, 1980.

———. *The Farthest Shore*. New York: Atheneum, 1972.

———. *Tehanu: The Last Book of Earthsea*. New York: Macmillan, 1990.

———. *The Tombs of Atuan*. New York: Atheneum, 1971.

———. *A Wizard of Earthsea*. New York: Bantam, 1975.

Lemon, Mark. *The Enchanted Doll and Tinykin's Transformations*. New York: Garland, 1976.

L'Engle, Madeleine. *An Acceptable Time*. New York: Dell, 1989.

———. *Dragons in the Water*. New York: Farrar, Straus & Giroux, 1976.

———. *Many Waters*. New York: Farrar, Straus & Giroux, 1986.

———. *A Ring of Endless Light*. New York: Farrar, Straus & Giroux, 1980.

———. *A Swiftly Tilting Planet*. New York: Farrar, Straus & Giroux, 1978.

———. *A Wind in the Door*. New York: Farrar, Straus & Giroux, 1973.

———. *A Wrinkle in Time*. New York: Farrar, Straus & Giroux, 1962.

———. *The Young Unicorns*. New York: Farrar, Straus & Giroux, 1968.

Lesser, Rika. *Hansel and Gretel*. Illus. Paul O. Zelinsky. New York: Putnam, 1984.

Lewis, C. S. *The Last Battle*. New York: Macmillan, 1956.

———. *The Lion, the Witch, and the Wardrobe*. New York: Macmillan, 1951.

———. *The Magician's Nephew*. New York: Macmillan, 1970.

———. *The Voyage of the Dawn Treader*. New York: Macmillan, 1952.

Linklater, Eric. *The Gold Dust Letters*. New York: Orchard Books, 1994.

———. *The Wind on the Moon*. New York: Macmillan, 1944.

Lively, Penelope. *The House in Norham Gardens*. New York: Dutton, 1974.

———. *The Revenge of Samuel Stokes*. New York: Dutton, 1981.

——. *A Stitch in Time*. New York: Dutton, 1976.

——. *The Whispering Knights*. New York: Dutton, 1976.

Lobel, Arnold. *Fables*. New York: Harper, 1980.

Lofting, Hugh. *The Story of Doctor Dolittle*. New York: Lippincott, 1920.

Louie, Ai-Ling. *Yeh-Shen*. Illus. Ed Young. New York: Philomel, 1982.

Lunn, Janet. *The Root Cellar*. New York: Scribner, 1983.

——. *Twin Spell*. New York: Harper, 1969.

McCaffery, Anne. *Dragondrums*. New York: Atheneum, 1979.

——. *Dragonsong*. New York: Atheneum, 1976.

——. *Dragonstar*. New York: Atheneum, 1977.

——. *Moreta: Dragon Lady of Pern*. New York: Ballantine, 1983.

——. *The White Dragon*. New York: Ballantine, 1978.

McDermott, Gerald. *Arrow to the Sun*. New York: Puffin, 1974.

MacDonald, George. *At the Back of the North Wind*. New York: Macmillan, 1964.

——. *The Princess and Curdie*. New York: Macmillan, 1945.

——. *The Princess and the Goblin*. New York: Penguin, 1964.

McHargue, Georgess. *Stoneflight*. New York: Viking, 1975.

McKinley, Robin. *Beauty: A Retelling of the Story of Beauty & the Beast*. New York: Harper Collins, 1978.

——. *The Blue Sword*. New York: Greenwillow, 1982.

——. *The Hero and the Crown*. New York: Greenwillow, 1984.

——. *The Outlaws of Sherwood*. New York: Greenwillow, 1988.

Mahy, Margaret. *The Changeover*. New York: Atheneum, 1984.

——. *Dangerous Spaces*. New York: Puffin, 1991.

——. *The Haunting*. New York: Atheneum, 1982.

——. *The Tricksters*. New York: McElderry, 1987.

Major, Kevin. *Blood Red Ochre*. New York: Delacorte, 1989.

Malotki, Ekkehart. *The Mouse Couple*. Illus. Michael Lacapa. Singapore: Northland, 1988.

Marshall, James. *Hansel and Gretel*. New York: Dial, 1990.

——. *Red Riding Hood*. New York: Dial, 1987.

Martin, Rafe. *Foolish Rabbit's Big Mistake*. Illus. Ed Young. New York: Putnam, 1985.

——. *The Rough-Face Girl*. Illus. David Shannon. New York: Putnam, 1992.

Mayne, William. *Earthfasts*. New York: Dutton, 1967.

——. *A Game of Dark*. New York: Dutton, 1971.

Mikolaycak, Charles. *Babushka*. New York: Holiday House, 1984.

Molesworth, Mary. *The Cuckoo Clock*. New York: Dutton, 1954.

——. *The Tapestry Room*. New York: Dutton, 1954.

Morimoto, Junko. *Kojuro and the Bears*. Pymble, NSW, Australia: Angus & Robertson, 1991.

Naylor, Phyllis Reynolds. *The Witch Herself*. New York: Dell, 1978.

———. *The Witch Returns*. New York: Dell, 1992.

———. *Witch Water*. New York: Dell, 1977.

Nesbit, Edith. *The Book of Dragons*. New York: Looking Glass, (n.d.).

———. *The Children and It*. New York: Penguin, 1959.

———. *The Enchanted Castle*. New York: Dent, 1968.

———. *The Phoenix and the Carpet*. New York: Penguin, 1959.

———. *The Story of the Amulet*. New York: Penguin, 1959.

Newman, Robert. *The Shattered Stone*. New York: Atheneum, 1975.

Nichols, Beverley. *The Stream That Stood Still*. London: Fontana, 1975.

———. *The Tree That Sat Down*. London: Fontana, 1975.

Nichols, Ruth. *The Marrow of the World*. New York: Atheneum, 1972.

Nixon, Joan Lowry. *Whispers from the Dead*. New York: Delacorte, 1989.

Norton, Andre. *Fur Magic*. New York: Archway, 1978.

———. *Quag Keep*. New York: Atheneum, 1978.

———. *Steel Magic*. New York: Archway, 1978.

Norton, Mary. *The Borrowers*. New York: Harcourt, 1953.

O'Brien, Robert C. *Mrs. Frisbie and the Rats of NIMH*. New York: Atheneum, 1971.

Ormondroyd, Edward. *All in Good Time*. New York: Parnassus, 1975.

———. *Castaways on Long Ago*. New York: Parnassus, 1973.

———. *Time at the Top*. New York: Parnassus, 1963.

Oughton, Jerrie. *How the Stars Fell into the Sky*. Illus. Lisa Desimini. New York: Houghton Mifflin, 1992.

Park, Ruth. *Playing Beatie Bow*. New York: Atheneum, 1982.

Pearce, Philippa. *Tom's Midnight Garden*. New York: Lippincott, 1959.

Peck, Richard. *The Ghost Belonged to Me*. New York: Viking 1975.

———. *Ghosts I Have Been*. New York: Viking, 1977.

———. *Voices after Midnight*. New York: Delacorte, 1989.

Perrault, Charles. "The Blue Beard," "Little Red Riding-Hood," and "The Master Cat or Puss in Boots." *Histories or Tales of Past Times*. New York: Garland, 1977.

———. *Cinderella*. Trans. & Illus. Diane Goode. New York: Knopf, 1988.

———. *Puss in Boots*. Illus. Fred Marcellino. New York: Farrar, Straus & Giroux, 1990.

Pierce, Meredith Ann. *The Darkangel Trilogy. The Pearl of the Soul of the World*. New York: Little, Brown, 1990.

Pinkwater, D. Manus. *Wingman*. New York: Dodd, 1975.

Potter, Beatrix. *The Tale of Peter Rabbit*. London: Frederick Warne, 1902.

Proysen, Alf. *Mrs. Pepperpot to the Rescue*. New York: Pantheon, 1964.

Pullman, Philip. *The Amber Spyglass*. New York: Knopf, 2000.

———. *The Golden Compass*. New York: Knopf, 1996.

———. *The Ruby Smoke*. New York: Random House, 1985.

———. *Shadow in the North*. New York: Knopf, 1986.

———. *The Subtle Knife*. New York: Knopf, 1997.

———. *The Tiger in the Well*. New York: Random House, 1990.

Rogasky, Barbara. *Rapunzel*. Illus. Trina Schart Hyman. New York: Holiday House, 1982.

Rowland, Della. *Beauty and the Beast*. Illus. Barbara Lanza. New York: Contemporary Books, 1990.

Rowland, Jada. *Rapunzel*. New York: Contemporary Books, 1989.

———. *The Elves and the Shoemakers*. New York: Contemporary Books, 1989.

Rowling, J. K. *Harry Potter and the Chamber of Secrets*. New York: Scholastic, 1999.

———. *Harry Potter and the Goblet of Fire*. New York: Scholastic, 2000.

———. *Harry Potter and the Prisoner of Azkaban*. New York: Scholastic, 1999.

———. *Harry Potter and the Sorcerer's Stone*. New York: Scholastic, 1998.

Ruskin, John. *The King of the Golden River*. New York: Greenwillow, 1978.

Salten, Felix. *Bambi*. New York: Simon & Schuster, 1928.

San Souci, Robert. *The Legend of Scarface*. Illus. Daniel San Souci. New York: Trumpet, 1978.

———. *The Talking Eggs*. Illus. Jerry Pinkney. New York: Dial, 1989.

Sargent, Sarah. *Weird Henry Berg*. New York: Crown, 1980.

Sauer, Julia. *Fog Magic*. New York: Viking, 1943.

Schroeder, Alan. *Lily and the Wooden Bowl*. Illus. Yoriko Ito. New York: Delacorte, 1994.

Schroeder, Binnette. *Beauty and the Beast*. New York: Crown, 1986.

Scieszka, Jon. *The True Story of the 3 Little Pigs*. Illus. Lane Smith. New York: Penguin, 1989.

Selden, George. *The Cricket in Times Square*. New York: Farrar, Straus & Giroux, 1960.

———. *Tucker's Countryside*. New York: Farrar, Straus & Giroux, 1969.

Sendak, Maurice. *Outside Over There*. New York: Harper & Row, 1981.

Senn, Steve. *The Double Disappearance of Walter Fozbek*. New York: Hastings House, 1980.

Service, Pamela F. *Vision Quest*. New York: Ballantine, 1989.

———. *Wizard of Wind and Rock*. Illus. Laura Marshall. New York: Atheneum, 1990.

Sewell, Anna. *Black Beauty*. New York: H. M. Caldwell, 1894.

Sharp, Margery. *The Rescuers*. Boston: Little, Brown, 1959.

Sherburne, Zoa. *Why Have the Birds Stopped Singing?* New York: Morrow, 1974.

Siegel, Robert. *Alpha Centauri*. Westchester, Ill.: Cornerstone Books, 1980.

Silverberg, Robert. *Letter from Atlantis*. New York: Atheneum, 1990.

Sleator, William. *Among the Dolls*. Illus. Trina Schart Hyman. New York: Dutton, 1975.

———. *Duplicate*. New York: Dutton, 1988.

———. *Intersteller Pig*. New York: Penguin, 1984.

———. *Into the Dream*. Illus. Ruth Sanderson. New York: Trumpet, 1979.

Sloat, Teri. *The Eye of the Needle*. New York: Dutton, 1990.

Smith, Dodie. *The Hundred and One Dalmations*. New York: Viking, 1957.

Snyder, Zilpha. *Black and Blue Magic*. New York: Atheneum, 1972.

Steele, Mary. *Journey Outside*. New York: Viking, 1969.

Steig, William. *Sylvester and the Magic Pebble*. New York: Trumpet, 1969.

Stewart, Mary. *The Crystal Cave*. New York: Morrow, 1970.

———. *The Hollow Hills*. New York: Morrow, 1973.

———. *The Last Enchantment*. New York: Morrow, 1979.

———. *A Walk in Wolf Wood*. New York: Morrow, 1980.

———. *The Wicked Day*. New York: Morrow, 1984.

Stockton, Frank. *The Griffin and the Minor Canon*. New York: Holt, 1963.

Sutcliff, Rosemary. *The Light Beyond the Forest*. New York: Dutton, 1980.

———. *The Road to Camlann: The Death of King Arthur*. Illus. Shirley Felts. New York: Dutton, 1982.

———. *The Sword and the Circle: King Arthur and the Knights of the Round Table*. New York: Dutton, 1981.

Sweeney, Joyce. *The Dream Collector*. New York: Delacorte, 1989.

Tannen, Mary. *The Lost Legend of Finn*. New York: Knopf, 1982.

———. *The Wizard Children of Finn*. New York: Knopf, 1981.

Thackeray, William. *The Rose and the Ring*. New York: Avon, 1965.

Thurber, James. *Many Moons*. New York: Harcourt, 1943.

———. *The 13 Clocks*. Illus. Marc Simont. New York: Dell, 1990 (reprint).

Tolkien, J. R. R. *The Hobbit*. New York: Houghton, 1966 (reprint).

———. *The Lord of the Rings*. Winchester, Mass.: Allen & Unwin, 1979 (reprint).

Travers, Pamela. *Mary Poppins*. New York: Harcourt, 1962.

Tymn, Marshall B., Kenneth J. Zahorski, and Robert H. Boyer, *Fantasy Literature: A Core Collection and Reference Guide*. New York: R. R. Bowker, 1979.

Uttley, Alison. *A Traveler in Time*. New York: Viking, 1940.

Voigt, Cynthia. *Tree by Leaf*. New York: Atheneum, 1988.

———. *Wings of a Falcon*. New York: Scholastic, 1993.

154 ~ Bibliography

Waugh, Sylvia. *Mennyms*. New York: Avon, 1993.

Weir, Rosemary. *Albert the Dragon*. New York: Abelard-Schuman, 1961.

Westall, Robert. *The Devil on the Road*. New York: Greenwillow, 1979.

———. *The Watch House*. New York: Greenwillow, 1978.

———. *The Wind Eye*. New York: Greenwillow, 1977.

White Deer of Autumn. *Ceremony in the Circle of Life*. Illus. Daniel San Souci. Hillsburo, Ore.: Beyond Words Publishing, 1983.

White, E. B. *Charlotte's Web*. New York: Harper, 1952.

———. *Stuart Little*. New York: Harper, 1945.

White, T. H. *The Sword in the Stone*. New York: Dell, 1973.

Wilde, Oscar. *The Selfish Giant*. New York: Harvey, 1967.

Willard, Nancy. *Beauty and the Beast*. Illus. Barry Moser. New York: Harcourt Brace Jovanovich, 1992.

Williams, Jay. *The Hero from Otherwhere*. New York: Walck, 1972.

Williams (Bianco) Margery. *The Velveteen Rabbit*. New York: Doubleday, 1958.

Wilson, David Henry. *The Coachman Rat*. New York: Carrol & Grap, 1989.

Winter, Jeanette. *Follow the Drinking Gourd*. New York: Trumpet, 1988.

Wiseman, David. *Jeremy Visick*. Boston: Houghton Mifflin, 1981.

Wood, Audrey. *Heckedy Peg*. Illus. Don Wood. New York: Harcourt Brace Jovanovich, 1987.

———. *King Bidgood's in the Bathtub*. Illus. Don Wood. New York: Harcourt Brace Jovanovich, 1985.

Wrede, Patricia C. *Calling on Dragons*. New York: Harcourt Brace Jovanovich, 1990.

———. *Dealing with Dragons*. New York: Harcourt Brace Jovanovich, 1990.

———. *Searching for Dragons*. New York: Harcourt Brace Jovanovich, 1991.

———. *Talking to Dragons*. New York: Harcourt Brace Jovanovich, 1985.

Wright, Betty Ren. *Christina's Ghost*. New York: Scholastic, 1985.

———. *The Ghost in the Window*. New York: Scholastic, 1987.

———. *Ghosts Beneath Our Feet*. New York: Scholastic, 1984.

———. *The Ghosts of Mercy Manor*. New York: Scholastic, 1993.

Yagawa, Sumiko. *The Crane Wife*. Illus. Suekichi Akaba. New York: Mulberry, 1979.

Yep, Laurence. *Dragon Cauldron*. New York: HarperCollins, 1991.

———. *Dragon of the Lost Sea*. New York: HarperCollins, 1982.

———. *Dragon War*. New York: HarperCollins, 1992.

———. *Dragonwings*. New York: HarperCollins, 1975.

———. *Sweetwater*. New York: Harper, 1973.

Yolen, Jane. *Dragon's Blood*. New York: Delacorte, 1982.

———. *The Emperor and the Kit*. Illus. Ed Young. New York: World Publishing, 1967.

———. *The Girl Who Loved the Wind*. New York: Crowell, 1974.

———. *Heart's Blood*. New York: Delacorte, 1984.

———. *A Sending of Dragons*. New York: Delacorte, 1987.

———. "Wild Goose and Gander" in *Tales of Wonder*. New York: Schocken, 1983.

———. *Wings*. Illus. Dennis Nolan. New York: Harcourt Brace Jovanovich, 1991.

———. *Wizard's Hall*. New York: Harcourt Brace Jovanovich, 1991.

Young, Ed. *Lon Po Po*. New York: Philomel, 1989.

———. *Seven Blind Mice*. New York: Scholastic, 1992.

Zelinsky, Paul O. *Rumpelstiltskin*. New York: Dutton, 1986.

Zipes, Jack. ed. *The Outspoken Princess and the Gentle Knight*. Illus. Stephane Poulin. New York: Bantam, 1994.

Zwerger, Lisbeth. *Hansel and Gretel*. New York: Picture Book Studio, 1988.

For Further Reading
and Professional Growth

Aiken, Joan. *The Way to Write for Children*. New York: St. Martin's Press, 1982.

Alexander, Lloyd. "High Fantasy and Heroic Romance." *Horn Book Magazine*, vol. 47 (December 1971), 577, 584.

Applebee, Arthur. *The Child's Concept of Story*. Chicago: University of Chicago Press, 1978.

Arbuthnot, May Hill, and Mark Taylor, eds. *Time for New Magic*. Glenview, Ill.: Foresman, 1971.

Attebury, Brian I. *The Fantasy Tradition in American Literature: From Irving to Le Guin*. Bloomington: Indiana University Press, 1980.

Bell, Anthea. *E. Nesbit*. London: Bodley Head, 1966.

Bettelheim, Bruno. *The Uses of Enchantment: The Meaning and Importance of Fairytales*. New York: Random House, 1976.

Blount, Margaret. *Animal Land: The Creatures of Children's Fiction*. New York: Avon, 1977.

Bosma, Bette. *Fairy Tales, Fables, Legends, and Myths*. 2nd ed. New York: Teachers College Press, 1992.

Boyer, Robert H., and Kenneth J. Zahorski. *Fantasies on Fantasy: A Collection of Critical Reflections*. New York: Avon, 1984.

Britton, J. "The Role of Fantasy." *English in Education*, vol. 5, no. 3 (1971), 39–44.

Calvino, Italo. *Italian Folktales*. Trans. George Martin. New York: Pantheon, 1981.

Cameron, Eleanor. "Fantasy," in *The Green and Burning Tree*. Boston: Little, Brown, 1969, 3–134.

———. "High Fantasy: *A Wizard of Earthsea*." *Horn Book Magazine*, vol. 47 (December 1971), 129–38.

Campbell, Joseph. *The Power of Myth*. New York: Doubleday, 1988.

Cook, Elizabeth. *The Ordinary and the Fabulous*. Cambridge: Cambridge University Press, 1969.

Cooper, J. C. *Fairy Tales: Allegories of the Inner Life*. Wellingborough, Northamptonshire: Aquarian, 1983.

Cott, Jonathan, ed. *Beyond the Looking Glass. Extraordinary Works of Fantasy and Fairy Tales*. New York: Stonehill, 1973.

Cox, Harvey. *The Feast of Fools. A Theological Essay on Festivity and Fantasy*. Cambridge, Mass.: Harvard University Press, 1969.

Crouch, Marcus. *The Nesbit Tradition: Children's Novels 1945–1972*. Totowa, N.J.: Rowman & Littlefield, 1972.

Cullinan, Bernice, and Lee Galda. *Literature and the Child*. 3rd ed. New York: Harcourt Brace College Publishers, 1994.

Darnton, Robert. "Peasants Tell Tales: The Meaning of Mother Goose," in *The Great Cat Massacre and Other Episodes in French Cultural History*. New York: Basic Books, 1984, 9–72.

Favat, F. André. *Child and Tale: The Origins of Interest*. Urbana, Ill.: NCTE, 1977.

Frye, Northrop. *The Educated Imagination*. Bloomington: Indiana University Press, 1964.

Hallett, Martin, and Barbara Karasek, eds. *Folk and Fairy Tales*. Lewiston, N.Y.: Broadview Press, 1991.

Harding, D. W. "Psychological Processes in the Reading of Fiction." In *The Cool Web: The Pattern of Children's Reading*. Edited by Margaret Meek, Aidan Warlow, and Griselda Barton. New York: Atheneum, 1978, 58–72.

Haviland, Virginia, ed. *Children and Literature: Views and Reviews*. Glenview, Ill.: Scott, Foresman, 1973.

Heisig, James W. "Bruno Bettelheim and the Fairy Tales." *Children's Literature*, vol. 6 (1977), 93–114.

Helson, Ravenna. "The Psychological Origins of Fantasy for Children in Mid-Victorian England." *Children's Literature*, vol. 3 (1974), 66–76.

———. "Fantasy and Self-Discovery." *Horn Book Magazine*, vol. 46 (1970), 121–34.

———. "Through the Pages of Children's Books." *Psychology Today*, vol. 7, no. 6 (1973), 107–17.

Higgins, James E. *Beyond Words: Mystical Fancy in Children's Literature*. New York: Teachers College Press, 1970.

Irwin, William R. *The Game of the Impossible: A Rhetoric of Fantasy*. Champaign: University of Illinois Press, 1976.

Jackson, Rosemary. *Fantasy: The Literature of Subversion*. London and New York: Methuen, 1981.

King, Stephen. *Danse Macabre*. New York: Everest House, 1981.

Kirkpatrick, D. L., ed. *Twentieth-Century Children's Writers*. 2nd ed. New York: St. Martin's Press, 1983.

Lanes, Selma G. *Down the Rabbit Hole: Adventures & Misadventures in the Realm of Children's Literature*. New York: Atheneum, 1972.

Le Guin, Ursula. "The Child and the Shadow," in *The Language of the Night: Essays in Fantasy and Science Fiction*. New York: Perigee, 1979.

Lehr, Susan, ed. *Battling Dragons: Issues and Controversy in Children's Literature*. Portsmouth, N.H.: Heinemann, 1995.

Lewis, C. S. "It All Began with a Picture. . . ." In *On Stories and Other Essays on Literature*. Edited by Walter Hooper. New York: Harcourt, 1982, 53–54.

Lockhead, Marion. *Renaissance of Wonder in Children's Literature*. Edinburgh: Canongate Publishing, 1977.

Lüthi, Max. *Once Upon a Time: On the Nature of Fairy Tales*. New York: Ungar, 1970.

Lynn, Ruth Nadelman. *Fantasy for Children: An Annotated Checklist and Reference Guide*. 2nd ed. New York: R. R. Bowker, 1983.

MacDonald, Ruth. "The Tale Retold: Feminist Fairy Tales." *CHLA Quarterly* 7, no. 2 (1982): 18–20.

Manlove, C. N. *Modern Fantasy: Five Studies*. New York: Cambridge University Press, 1975.

———. *The Impulse of Fantasy Literature*. Kent, Ohio: Kent State University Press, 1983.

Miller, Patricia. "The Importance of Being Earnest: The Fairy Tale in 19th-century England." *CHLA Quarterly* 7, no. 2 (1982): 11–14.

Molson, Francis J. "Children's Fantasy and Science Fiction." In *The Science Fiction Reference Book*. Edited by Marshall Tymn. Mercer Island, Wash.: Starmont House, 1981.

———. "The Earthsea Trilogy: Ethical Fantasy for Children." In *Ursula K. Le Guin: Voyager to Inner Lands and to Outer Space*. Edited by Joe DeBolt. Port Washington, N.Y.: Kennikat Press, 1979.

Mousatakis, Christina, ed. "Fairy Tales: Their Staying Power." *CHLA Quarterly* 7, no. 2 (1982):1–36.

Nilsen, Aileen Pace, and Kenneth Donelson. *Literature for Today's Young Adult*. 4th ed. New York: HarperCollins, 1993.

Opie, Iona, and Peter Opie. *The Classic Fairy Tales*. London: Oxford University Press, 1974.

Paterson, Katherine. *The Spying Heart: More Thoughts on Reading and Writing Books for Children*. New York: Dutton, 1989.

Pflieger, Pat. *A Reference Guide to Modern Fantasy for Children*. Westport, Conn.: Greenwood Press, 1984.

Pitcher, Evelyn, and Ernst Prellinger. *Children Tell Stories: An Analysis of Fantasy*. New York: International Universities Press, 1963.

Prickett, Stephen. *Victorian Fantasy*. Bloomington: Indiana University Press, 1979.

Propp, Vladimir. *Morphology of the Folktale*. Trans. Laurence Scott. 2nd ed. Austin: Universtity of Texas Press, 1968.

Rees, David. *The Marble in the Water: Essays on Contemporary Writers of Fiction for Children and Young Adults*. Boston: Horn Book, 1980.

Sale, Roger. *Fairy Tales and After: From Snow White to E. B. White*. Cambridge, Mass.: Harvard University Press, 1978.

Schlobin, Rogar C., ed. *The Aesthetics of Fantasy Literature and Art*. Notre Dame, Ind.: University of Notre Dame Press, 1982.

Tolkien, J. R. R. "On Fairy Stories," in *Tree and Leaf*. Boston: Houghton, 1965.

Townsend, John Rowe. *A Sense of Story: Essays on Contemporary Writers for Children*. Philadelphia: Lippincott, 1971.

Tymn, Marshall, Kenneth J. Zahorski, and Robert H. Boyer. *Fantasy Literature. A Core Collection and Reference Guide*. New York: R. R. Bowker, 1979.

Waggoner, Diana. *The Hills of Faraway: A Guide to Fantasy*. New York: Atheneum, 1978.

Yolen, Jane. *Touch Magic: Fantasy, Faerie and Folklore in the Literature of Childhood*. New York: Philomel, 1981.

Zipes, Jack. *Breaking the Magic Spell: Radical Theories of Folk and Fairy Tales*. Austin: University of Texas Press, 1979.

Index

~

About the Authors

Pamela Gates is professor of English at Central Michigan University and is currently serving as associate dean of the College of Humanities and Social & Behavioral Sciences at CMU. Dr. Gates finished her doctoral work at Michigan State University in 1993, where she specialized in literacy and learning, literature for children and young adults, language arts, and English education. She has taught a wide range of courses over the past sixteen years, including children's literature, fantasy literature for children, young adult literature, multicultural literature for children, heroic traditions in literature for children, and graduate seminars in children's literature. Dr. Gates has worked extensively with professional development school initiatives in public schools, serves as cochair of the Michigan Storytelling Festival, and is assistant editor of the *Language Arts Journal of Michigan*. She has presented nationally and internationally, has published more than a dozen articles and book chapters, and is currently completing a second resource book featuring multicultural literature for children and young adults.

Francis Molson is professor emeritus of English, having retired from Central Michigan University in 1997 after twenty-five years of teaching—the last ten serving as chair of the department. Dr. Molson did his doctoral work at Notre Dame and worked and taught at Indiana University–South Bend for fifteen years before coming to CMU. Dr. Molson has presented nationally and internationally and is widely published, with over fifty papers, articles, and books to his credit. An avid collector of art from children's illustrators, Dr. Molson and his wife, Mary Lois, have established and donated an extensive art collection to the Clark Historical Library at Central Michigan University's Park Library.

Susan Steffel is professor of English at Central Michigan University and a veteran teacher with thirty years of teaching experience. Dr. Steffel completed her doctorate at Michigan State University in 1993 with specialties in reading and writing theory, literacy, young adult literature, and English education. Before coming to CMU, she spent eighteen years teaching writing, reading, and literature in the public schools. Currently, Dr. Steffel teaches English education courses in composition methods, reading methods, and young adult literature. She continues to work in the public schools, providing inservice training to teachers around the state in the areas of young adult literature, reading and writing across the curriculum, authentic assessment, and aligning curriculum with current standards and benchmarks. Dr. Steffel has presented nationally and internationally and published articles and book chapters, as well as dozens of book reviews of young adult literature. She has received numerous awards for her teaching, including the Excellence in Teaching Award in 1996. She was nominated for the Carnegie U.S. Professor of the Year in 1997, and received the Edwin Towle Professorship in 1998. Dr. Steffel serves as coeditor of the *Language Arts Journal of Michigan* and is president-elect of the Michigan Council of Teachers of English.